# HeadStart
## Primary

# English Reading Comprehension

## Success in
# Year 4

GARDEN HOUSE SCHOOL
TURKS ROW
LONDON
SW3 4TW
020 7730 1652

Written and illustrated
by Jim Edmiston

HeadStart ✓
Primary

## Acknowledgements:

**Author:** Jim Edmiston
**Cover Design:** Jim Edmiston and Kathryn Webster

The right of Jim Edmiston to be identified as the author of this publication has been asserted by him in accordance with the Copyright, Designs and Patents Act 1988.

HeadStart Primary Ltd
Elker Lane
Clitheroe
BB7 9HZ

**T.** 01200 423405
**E.** info@headstartprimary.com
**www.headstartprimary.com**

All rights reserved. No part of this publication may be reproduced, stored in a retrieval system, or transmitted in any form or by any means, electronic, mechanical, photocopying, recording or otherwise without the prior permission of the publisher.

Published by HeadStart Primary Ltd 2019 © **HeadStart Primary Ltd 2019**

A record for this book is available from the British Library -
**ISBN: 978-1-908767-35-6**

# Year 4

## CONTENTS

Test Administration Guidance

SCALED SCORE TEST A
Fishface Freddie and Monsters of the Deep / Whale Diary / A Guide to Whales

SCALED SCORE TEST B
Paper Aeroplanes / Icarus / Kites

SCALED SCORE TEST C
Street Party / Flags and Everything / The Dark Horse

Answers, Mark Schemes and Progress Tracking/Scaled Score Information

© Copyright HeadStart Primary Ltd

V3

# INTRODUCTION

**HeadStart Primary** English Reading Comprehension has been produced to make the teacher's formative assessment of reading as straightforward as possible. At the same time, its aim is to develop children's reading skills and encourage their engagement with literature in all its forms.

With this in mind, sections have been organised to follow closely the National Curriculum and the different reading skills (content domains) highlighted in the KS2 English Reading Test Framework 2016 (available to download at www.gov.uk), with an emphasis on **comprehension, making inferences, language for effect** and **themes and conventions**.

The tasks presented here increase in difficulty as you work through a section. This allows for:

- easier access for the child still acquiring and developing basic skills

- a challenge for the child whose skills are more secure

- a further challenge and consolidation for the child who is in the process of exceeding year group expectations.

This structure enables the teacher to monitor the progress a child is making in each particular skill area and, as a result, will ease the process of formative assessment and subsequent planning. An individual child, for instance, may have a wide vocabulary but lack inferential skills. The organisation of tasks will make this apparent so that the child's learning can be moved forward.

A range of fiction and non-fiction underpins the reading tasks as well as the range of texts in the **TESTS** section. Since the removal of national curriculum levels, schools are now free to choose their own methods of monitoring progress in reading. The tests here have been provided to help the process of formative assessment, but they could be used simply as further practice tasks or to allow children to glimpse a test format. This is for the professional judgement of the class teacher.

(Similarly, two tasks involving identifying the difference between fact and opinion, though not part of the Year 4 curriculum, are included as a possible challenge for some children.)

For complete flexibility, the accompanying CD-ROM includes not only a copy of the book in colour for use on the interactive whiteboard, but also an answer book.

Finally, the texts have been chosen in relation to Year 4 subject areas, their age-appropriate spelling lists and with the enjoyment of reading in mind.

## Words in context

Strand:     Comprehension

National Curriculum reference:

- checking that the text makes sense to them

Reading Test / Content Domain links:   2a, 2b

## WHAT DOES IT MEAN?

Think of another word or phrase that means the same as, or is similar to, the one in **bold**. Looking at the rest of the sentence will help you. One has already been done for you.

1.  The ship was lost in the **mist**.                    _____

2.  Climbing a mountain is **risky**.                    _____

3.  The monster was **enormous**.                    _____

4.  The birds started to sing at **dawn**.          _____ sunrise _____

5.  What time will the visitors **arrive**?          _____

6.  The arrow hit the **centre** of the target.    _____

7.  The puzzle was very **difficult**.                _____

8.  Try to **imagine** your favourite holiday.    _____

9.  **Perhaps** I'll go to the cinema tonight.    _____

10. Do you **possess** a ball I can borrow?      _____

11. The teacher was **pleased** with her class. _____

12. The soldier was very **courageous**.          _____

## HOW TO BE GOOD

The word **good** can mean all sorts of things.  Here are some sentences that contain the word **good**.  What does it mean in these sentences? Draw a line linking each one to its meaning.  One has already been done for you.

1.   If you are **good**, I'll take you to the seaside.

2.   The baker's pies are really **good**.

3.   The team needs to find some **good** players.

4.   Hammers are very **good** for banging in nails.

5.   It's important to have a **good** breakfast.

6.   Is under the bed a **good** place to keep your money?

7.   It's **good** of you to give money to charity.

8.   Pudding is served with a **good** amount of cream.

safe

useful

well-behaved

kind

delicious

healthy

large

talented

# ENGLISH CAN BE CONFUSING

Some words are spelt the same but mean different things.  It helps to see them in a sentence.  Look at the words in **bold**.  Tick the correct meaning.

1.    My cousin is an amazing **sewer**.

   someone who sews ◯          drain ◯

2.    My sister is a wonderful **drawer**.

   someone who draws ◯          box-like container ◯

3.    When we went out for a picnic, there was nowhere to **park**.

   public space with trees ◯          leave a car somewhere ◯

4.    When I'm older, I'm going to be a **rock** star.

   type of music ◯          type of stone ◯

5.    We stopped rowing the boat and tied it to the **bank**.

   place to keep your money ◯          side of a river ◯

6.    The prisoner escaped through the bars using a **file**.

   tool for cutting metal ◯          collection of documents ◯

7.    Billy is a wonderful **jumper**.

   woolly sweater ◯          someone who jumps ◯

# CAPTAIN NELL AND FISHFACE FREDDIE

Here are some sentences with key words.

Not only did Captain Nell have lots of experience at sea, she was also a courageous pirate. Unfortunately, her crew included Fishface Freddie, who accidentally dropped a heavy cannonball on his big, clumsy feet.

1. Which word or phrase tells you that Captain Nell knew how to sail her ship?

   _____ ✏

2. Which word tells you that Fishface Freddie didn't mean to drop the cannonball?

   _____ ✏

3. Was Captain Nell brave? Write down the word that tells you.

   _____ ✏

4. Use some of the words in the box to make sense of this paragraph.

   After weeks at sea, they _____ reached

   the long-lost, treasure island, where they started digging

   _____. Nell and Freddie dug and dug

   until their hands were _____ and sore, but

   by sundown they had uncovered the buried treasure chest.

   | easily | sandy |
   |--------|-------|
   | now | eventually |
   | basically | tried |
   | well | frantically |
   | blistered | first |

---

Use the rest of the sentence to work out the meaning of the words in bold.
Put a tick in the circle next to your answer.

1. | It was in Captain Nell's **nature** to be patient.

In this sentence, does **nature** mean:

animals and plants ◯

character ◯

hospital ◯

2. | Fishface Freddie wasn't good at **obeying orders.**

In this sentence, does **obeying orders** mean:

being a waiter ◯

sailing the ship ◯

doing as he was told ◯

3. | Captain Nell **divided up** the treasure fairly.

In this sentence, does **divided up** mean:

shared it out ◯

broke it into pieces ◯

hid it somewhere safe ◯

4. | They were **disappointed** when they opened the chest.

In this sentence, does **disappointed** mean:

had an appointment ◯

sad and upset ◯

tired and hungry ◯

5. | Finding dog biscuits and false teeth inside the chest, Freddie was **delighted.**

In this sentence, does **delighted** mean:

underneath a light ◯

very pleased ◯

lost weight ◯

## FIND A WORD

In these paragraphs from fairytales there are some words for you to find.

Jack gazed up at the clouds and tried to imagine what it was like in the giant's castle. Clara, their one and only cow, munched the grass. She was very content. Jack disliked the idea of taking her to market to be sold.

Find words that mean the same as these:

looked                    _____

picture in your mind      _____

ate                       _____

happy                     _____

hated                     _____

Cinderella was pleased at last to have the house to herself, even though she was miserable about not going to the ball. She grumbled about all the work she still had to do before the ugly sisters returned. If only she had a fairy godmother, she would be so grateful.

Find words that mean the same as these:

glad        _____

sad         _____

groaned     _____

came back   _____

thankful    _____

## WOLF AND HARE

Read this text about Wolf and Hare and think carefully about the answers.

A southerly breeze whispered across the long grass at the edge of Rainbow Wood. Hungry, Wolf emerged from the trees. Meanwhile, Hare was feeding on its own, its sharp ears listening out for predators.  The sound of Wolf getting closer was unmistakable. Hare stopped eating and crouched, frozen to the spot. Old Wolf sniffed the air, howled only inches away and headed home.

1.    What do you think the writer means by saying the hare was **frozen to the spot**?  Put a circle round one of the answers that means the same:

stuck          scared          cold          solid

2.    Choose a word or phrase that means the same as **emerged**.  Tick **one** box.

ran quickly ☐

disappeared ☐

came out ☐

strolled ☐

3.    Which phrase tells you that Hare had good hearing? _____

4.    Which word suggests Hare has met Wolf before? _____

# Explaining words in context

Strand:    Comprehension

National Curriculum reference:

- [checking that the text makes sense to them], discussing their understanding, and explaining the meaning of words in context

Reading Test / Content Domain links:   2a, 2b, 2f

## TRICKY WORDS

These words in **bold** need the other words in the sentence to show you what they mean. Tick one of the meanings and explain why you chose your answer.

1. When I saw the king, I removed my hat and gave a **bow**.

   **bending down respectfully** ◯   **archer's weapon** ◯   **tied ribbon** ◯

   WHY? _____

   _____

2. The angry people on the boat were having a **row**.

   **use oars to propel a boat** ◯   **quarrel** ◯

   WHY? _____

   _____

3. Day and night, the children searched the skies for the **bat**.

   **cricketer's equipment** ◯   **flying mammal** ◯

   WHY? _____

   _____

4. Mum is always trying to stop our baby **putting** balls in his mouth.

   **placing** ◯   **hit with a putter in golf** ◯

   WHY? _____

   _____

5. Caught on the thorn bushes, my t-shirt was covered in **tears**.

water drops from the eye ◯     rips ◯

WHY? _____

_____


6. Leilah's torch gave off such a **brilliant** light it almost blinded me.

very bright ◯         exciting ◯

WHY? _____

_____


7. Matt **treasured** the signed football from his favourite team.

buried in a hole in the ground ◯     looked after carefully ◯

WHY? _____

_____


8. Suddenly, the baby in the supermarket broke into a loud **bawl**.

round, bouncy toy ◯     container for food ◯     cry ◯

WHY? _____

_____


9. During the **reign** of King Drizzle, the weather was awful every day.

period of time on the throne ◯     wet weather ◯

WHY? _____

_____

# THE GODS OF ANCIENT GREECE

**Zeus** was the god of the sky and thunder. He was king of the gods, able to unleash his thunderbolt if he ever encountered a situation that angered or caused him annoyance.

**Hephaestus** was the god of blacksmiths, fire and volcanoes. He worked in his own palace on Mount Olympus, forging winged helmets, weapons, and chariots for other gods.

**Athena** was the goddess of wisdom, civilisation, art and justice. Because of her unique qualities, Greeks worshipped her as the protector of the ancient city of Athens.

**Aphrodite** was known as the goddess of love. But, fearing that her beauty might easily lead to war, Zeus had her married to Hephaestus, who was thought to be hideous.

**Apollo,** the son of Zeus, was the god of prophecy, music, poetry and truth, and was portrayed as an athletic youth. People turned to him for healing and protection from evil.

**Hermes** could fly quickly between the gods on Olympus and humans on Earth. Often sculpted with wings on his helmet or sandals, he was the messenger of the gods.

Now go to the next page and answer the questions. Remember you can come back and check the text for clues at any time.

1. Match each word to one that means the opposite.  One has been done for you.

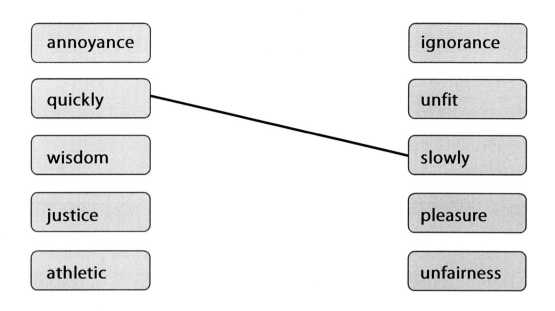

| annoyance | | ignorance |
| quickly | | unfit |
| wisdom | | slowly |
| justice | | pleasure |
| athletic | | unfairness |

2. In the descriptions of the Greek gods, find words that mean the following:

| Meaning | Word |
| --- | --- |
| met or came across | |
| only one of its kind | |
| creating something by heating and hammering | |
| very ugly | |
| a prediction of a future event | |

3. Can you think of other words for these?

thunderbolt _____

ancient _____

fearing _____

© Copyright HeadStart Primary Ltd

# PANDORA'S BOX

Zeus ordered Hephaestus to create Pandora, the first woman on Earth. The gods gave her many gifts: Athena clothed her, Apollo gave her musical ability, Aphrodite gave her beauty and Hermes gave her speech.

But the king of the gods was so cunning. He gave her hand in marriage to the gentle, kind-hearted Epimetheus in order to seek revenge on his brother, Prometheus for giving fire to humans.

Zeus presented Pandora with a box, a key and a note that warned against opening it. Tragically, curiosity got the better of her. Pandora lifted the lid. All at once, all that was destructive escaped into the world: death, sickness, envy and war. Only one thing remained and that was HOPE.

## Was it a Box?

The original Greek word was **pithos**. It wasn't a box, but an immense jar, often big enough for someone to fit inside. It was used for the storage of wine, oil, grain and other provisions. It was similar in height to a man.

Choose a word from the box below to complete these sentences:

1.   Someone with a **cunning** plan would be quite _____

2.   A **kind-hearted** person is likely to be _____

3.   Anything **destructive** in the world would be _____

4.   Someone suffering from **envy** would feel _____

5.   A jar that was **immense** would be _____

6.   If you were sent out for **provisions**, you'd buy _____

| | | | | |
|---|---|---|---|---|
| careless | friendly | heavy | pots | enormous |
| overjoyed | crafty | groceries | weak | generous |
| damaging | lonely | jealous | exhausted | heroic |

# PEOPLE SAY SOME FUNNY THINGS

Read what Naomi says about being invited to join the school swimming team.

It was supposed to be a secret, but my brother, Ben, let the cat out of the bag. Of all the kids they could have chosen for the team, they plumped for yours truly. Not only that, I was to captain the team. Now that was the icing on the cake! Ben wanted that place, so he started to cry. Only crocodile tears, of course. He was making a mountain out of a molehill. The day arrived. I nearly got cold feet. When I pulled back the curtains, I could see it was raining cats and dogs. That didn't help. I knew I'd be in hot water if I didn't turn up. But I was there in a jiffy and the school came out on top.

| phrase | meaning |
|---|---|
| let the cat out of the bag | |
| plumped for | |
| yours truly | |
| the icing on the cake | |
| crocodile tears | |
| making a mountain out of a molehill | |
| got cold feet | |
| raining cats and dogs | |
| in a jiffy | |
| came out on top | |

© Copyright HeadStart Primary Ltd

© Copyright HeadStart Primary Ltd

## Retrieving and recording information

Strand:     Comprehension

National Curriculum reference:

- retrieving and recording information / identifying key details
  from fiction and non-fiction

Reading Test / Content Domain links:   2a, 2b

# SEED DISPERSAL

Read through this information about plants and the different ways they rely on to scatter their seeds. Then check the information for answers to the questions.

### Dandelions

Dandelion seeds are attached to fine, fluffy hairs which are blown some distance by the wind or by children playing at 'telling the time'. This is a very successful way of dispersing seeds.

### Sycamore

The seeds of sycamore trees are shaped like wings or propellers. When they fall or are blown from the tree, the wind carries them spinning far away from the shade of the tree.

### Hazel

Squirrels like to eat hazelnuts as well as store them for the winter when there is less food around. Often they forget where they buried them, allowing the nuts to grow into new plants.

### Coconuts

Coconuts can be carried off by a river or the tide. Their tough skin protects them from salt water for up to two months. Ocean currents can take them thousands of miles before they are washed up on land and start to grow.

### Lupins

Lupin seeds are found inside a pod. As the pod dries out, the side facing the sun dries faster, causing the pod to buckle and twist until it pops open. This sends the seeds away to new fertile ground.

### Burrs

The seeds of burrs are covered in tiny spines or hooks which hitch a ride on the fur of passing animals or the clothing of human beings. Later, when the seeds are rubbed or scratched off, they fall to the ground.

1.  Which **two** plants rely on the wind to spread their seeds?

    _____

2.  How does having a thick skin help the coconut find somewhere to grow?

    _____

    _____

3.  Which **two** plants often get help from human beings?

    _____

4.  Which **two** plants rely on animals to disperse their seeds?

    _____

5.  How are burrs carried to new ground away from the parent plant?

    _____

    _____

6.  How is the wind useful to the sycamore tree?

    _____

    _____

7.  The lupin is a flower that has a special way of dispersing its seeds.  How does it
    happen?

    _____

    _____

8.  Write **two** phrases that show how important it is for seeds to grow away from
    the main plant.

    _____

    _____

## THE WEATHER

Those people who work outside or at sea have always been affected by the weather. So it isn't surprising that we have tried in different ways to forecast sunshine, rain, fog or snow. This is especially true for our British Isles, here on the edge of the Atlantic. There have been many attempts to predict the weather, from using seaweed to computers.

1.     Whose work is likely to be affected by bad weather?

_____

_____

2.     Why might we in the British Isles be interested in the weather forecast?

_____

3.     Name **two** ways that people have tried to predict the weather.

_____

Many governments now provide forecasts, warnings and advice to the public in order to protect life and property and help people running businesses. Not only will severe weather ruin your family picnic, thunderstorms can cause damage to property, power cuts, flooding and problems with transport.

1.     By providing weather forecasts, how do governments help people?

_____

_____

2.     As well as spoiling your day out, what other damage might storms cause?

_____

_____

# WEIRD AND WONDERFUL TRADITIONS

Long before the computer age, there were rhymes about the weather.

*If in the sky*

*you see cliffs and towers,*

*it won't be long*

*before there are showers*

This can be quite accurate. When clouds stretch up like cliffs and towers, it's a sign that the air is not very settled, leading to wet weather and sometimes thunder.

1. If you see clouds that look like castles and towers, what does it say about the air? _____

2. What kind of weather might you expect? _____

_____

*Oak before ash, we're in for a splash.*

*Ash before oak, we're in for a soak.*

Will leaves appear on oak trees before ash trees, or the other way around? This is supposed to predict the amount of rain we can expect: small splash or a huge soak. It's a great rhyme, and, if it's said often enough, people might believe it. Unfortunately, there is no scientific evidence for it at all.

1. Which part of oak and ash trees are supposed to predict the weather?

_____

2. Even if it's not true, what might make people believe it?

_____

## A COW WITH ITS TAIL TO THE WEST MAKES THE WEATHER THE BEST.

## A COW WITH ITS TAIL TO THE EAST MAKES THE WEATHER THE LEAST.

Animals such as cows often eat grass with the wind behind them. If there are predators nearby, the wind will carry their scent towards the grazing cows. They will be facing the right direction for running away. Westerly winds tend to bring fair weather; east winds tend to bring bad weather. So this could be partly true. But, oh dear! What do you do if the cows are all facing different directions?

1. How does the wind help animals to stay safe?

   _____

   _____

2. What sort of weather do we tend to have when the wind comes from the west?

   _____

3. When the weather is bad, what direction does the wind tend to come from?

   _____

4. Do you think this is an accurate way of forecasting the weather?

   _____

5. The rhyme uses the phrase **makes the weather the least**. What does **least** mean here?

   _____

# RED SKY AT NIGHT, SHEPHERD'S DELIGHT.

# RED SKY IN THE MORNING, SHEPHERD'S WARNING.

This is usually true. If the sky to the west starts to glow red when the sun is setting, it means the air is clear enough for us to see the sun's rays. Warm weather in Britain comes from the west. A red sky in the morning can be caused by the dawn light from the east reflecting off ice crystals high among rain clouds. Not so good.

1.  Why might a shepherd be delighted if he saw a red sky at night?

_____

2.  What can we say about the air when the sky glows red in the evening?

_____

3.  Does our warm weather come from the east or the west?

_____

4.  In which direction would you look to see the sun rising?

_____

5.  Ice crystals reflect light. Name something else that reflects light.

_____

6.  Where are the ice crystals that are referred to in this text?

_____

# WINGS AND WINDS

Have you travelled on holiday by plane? Airlines are very interested in the weather. Fog – known as *low ceilings* – can prevent aircraft from landing and taking off. Turbulence (when strong winds give passengers a rough ride) is an in-flight hazard. Thunderstorms are a problem for all aircraft because they cause severe turbulence. Ice due to heavy rain, as well as large hail, strong winds and lightning, can cause severe damage to an aeroplane in flight. Volcanic ash, depending on the direction of the wind, is quite a serious problem as aeroplanes can lose engine power inside ash clouds.

1.   What do pilots mean when they talk about a *low ceiling*? _____

2.   Why might this be a problem? _____

_____

3.   What is **turbulence**? _____

_____

4.   Name **two** things that cause turbulence. _____

_____

5.   Why are active volcanoes a serious problem for aeroplanes? _____

_____

_____

# THE HISTORY OF FORECASTING

In ancient times, people tried to predict the weather by looking at the shapes of clouds and the flight of birds, as well as listening to the chirping of insects.

Things changed in the 18<sup>th</sup> century.

In 1774, Francis Beaufort was born in Ireland and became an officer in the Royal Navy. He developed what is known as the **Beaufort Scale** – a way of measuring the force of the wind.

Fishermen and sailors still use it today.

This is a scale that goes from **0 = calm** to **12 = hurricane**.

Some examples from the Beaufort Scale

- When the force of the wind is 0, the sea will be **calm like the surface of a mirror**.
- When it increases to 1, the surface of the sea will still be **calm but with ripples**.
- At 2, the sea will be **smooth but with wavelets**.
- But by the time the wind is storm force and gets up to 10 on the scale, waves will be **very high**.
- When it is 12, waves are described as **phenomenal**.

1. Describe **3** ways in which people tried to predict the weather before the 18<sup>th</sup> century.

_____

_____

_____

2. Where was Francis Beaufort born?

_____

3. What does the Beaufort Scale measure?

_____

4. Can you think of another word or phrase that means the same as **force**?

_____

5. Circle **one** group of people who use the Beaufort Scale today.

    police          doctors          sailors          fire fighters

6. If the wind were **Force 0**, what would the waves be like?

_____

7. Write down a word or phrase that means the same as **phenomenal**.

_____

# THE FIRST WEATHER FORECAST

In 1859, Robert FitzRoy, an English officer in the Royal Navy, was disturbed by the loss of a ship called the *Royal Charter* in a terrible storm. As a result, he developed weather charts to help ship captains at sea. He was the first to call this **weather forecasting**. This was quite different from using old rhymes to make a prophecy about the weather.

He was the first person to be made head of the Met Office, which produces weather forecasts for us today.

Sometimes, people laughed at the attempts of Beaufort and FitzRoy to take a scientific approach to weather patterns. But, in 1861, daily forecasts were printed in *The Times* newspaper.

One of the areas of the seas around the British Isles is now named after FitzRoy.

1.      What was the name of the ship that was lost in the storm in 1859?

_____

2.      How was **weather forecasting** different from **prophecy**?

_____

_____

3.      Where and when were the first weather forecasts seen by the public?

_____

# THE BEAUFORT SCALE

| Beaufort Number | Wind Speed (mph) | Wind Classification | Wind Effects on Land | Wind Effects on Water |
|---|---|---|---|---|
| 0 | 0 | Calm | Smoke rises vertically | Water calm like a mirror |
| 1 | 1-3 | Light air | Smoke drift shows wind direction | Ripples on water; no crests of foam |
| 2 | 4-7 | Light breeze | Leaves rustle, wind felt on face; weather vane moves | Small wavelets |
| 3 | 8-12 | Gentle breeze | Leaves and twigs constantly moving; flags begin to flap | Large wavelets; crests begin to break |
| 4 | 13-18 | Moderate breeze | Dust raised; small branches move | Small waves 1-4 feet; many whitecaps (foam) |
| 5 | 19-24 | Fresh breeze | Small trees begin to sway | Longer waves 4-8 feet; whitecaps common; spray |
| 6 | 25-31 | Strong breeze | Larger tree branches moving | Larger waves 8-13 feet; whitecaps common; more spray |
| 7 | 32-38 | Near gale | Whole trees moving; hard to walk against the wind | Sea heaps up; waves 13-20 feet; crest break |
| 8 | 39-46 | Gale | Twigs break off trees; hard to walk against the wind | Waves 13-20 feet and longer breaking into foam |
| 9 | 47-54 | Strong gale | Slight damage to buildings; tiles and slates torn off roof | High waves 20 feet; rolling seas; reduced visibility |
| 10 | 55-63 | Storm | Trees uprooted; serious damage to buildings | Waves 20-30 feet; crests overhanging; sea white |
| 11 | 64-72 | Violent storm | Widespread damage | Waves 30-45 feet; air filled with spray; reduced visibility |
| 12 | 73 + | Hurricane | Widespread destruction | Waves Over 45 feet; air filled with foam; forceful spray |

(To answer the following questions, you need to know that **wind classification** means how weather men and women describe the wind.)

© Copyright HeadStart Primary Ltd

1.  When the wave creates **small wavelets**, what is happening in the trees?

    _____

2.  When there is a **gentle breeze**, what might be happening to flags?

    _____

3.  What is the wind speed when the crests of waves begin to break?

    _____

4.  When waves are between one and four feet, what is the **Beaufort Number**?

    _____

5.  When dust starts to be raised, what will the wind be like?

    _____

6.  If you are at sea and begin to feel the sea spray on your face, what is the wind speed likely to be?

    _____

7.  What would it be like going to school in a **near gale**?

    _____

8.  When the wind is strong enough to damage your roof tiles, what is it like at sea?

    _____

    _____

9.  If a **near gale** turned into a **storm**, what would you see happening to trees?

    _____

    _____

Read this poem about the weather and answer the questions.

## Thunder Clap

When the thunder roars as loud as it's able
Ginger, our cat, hides under the table.
There's not much room as far as I can tell,
Especially when I'm hiding there as well.

My guinea pigs, Jenny, Benny and Lenny
Are not keen on lightning flashing and many
Of the gerbils, about six, scurry too
Under the table with you know who.

Nimbus, the dog, doesn't want to be last
And dives under too at the next thunder blast.
I'm pleased now, last week, on our trip to the zoo,
I didn't nag Mum for a pet kangaroo.

The thunder claps like a round of applause
At the sight of the tangle of forty-four paws,
Not to mention the one human being, that's me,
Struggling and squirming to get myself free.

The weather's been fine now for over an hour.
Not a whisper of wind or sign of a shower.
The sun is bright as ever it gets,
But here am I – stuck in a muddle of pets.

1.   Look at the 1ˢᵗ, 3ʳᵈ and the 4ᵗʰ verses. How is the thunder described differently?

_____

_____

2.   The writer is referred to as 'I' in the 1ˢᵗ verse. How is the writer referred to in the 2ⁿᵈ verse?

_____

3.   In the last 2 verses what words are used to describe the large number of pets?

_____

# Fact and opinion

Strand:    Comprehension

National Curriculum reference:

- retrieving and recording information from non-fiction
- distinguishing between statements of fact and opinion

Reading Test / Content Domain links:   2a, 2b, 2g

## OUR TEAM

A **fact** is true and can be proved. An **opinion** is how someone feels about something. Look at this conversation and circle **fact** or **opinion**.

United are the best football team.

**fact** or **opinion**

But City beat them last week!

**fact** or **opinion**

Even so, United are top of the league.

**fact** or **opinion**

They were lucky to get a penalty.

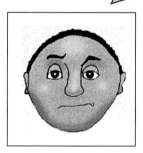

**fact** or **opinion**

The referee made the right decision.

**fact** or **opinion**

City have scored more goals than them.

**fact** or **opinion**

# PETS

Irena has come to the front of the class to talk about her pets. Some things she says are facts; some things are opinions. Write an **f** for fact or an **o** for opinion in the box under each speech bubble.

I have a cat, a dog and a tortoise.

They're all very cute.

Tortoises have a hard shell.

My cat, Spangle, has the softest fur.

Muggy, the dog, does tricks such as rolling over.

My tortoise, Arthur, can keep you amused for hours.

Grandad is going to buy me a chicken.

Then I'll have four pets altogether.

But I still won't have enough pets.

# The main idea

Strand:     Comprehension

National Curriculum reference:

- identifying main ideas drawn from more than one paragraph

Reading Test / Content Domain links:   2a, 2b, 2c, 2f

# HORSES AND PONIES

In the following paragraphs, one sentence is the **main idea**. The other two sentences contain **details** that tell you more about the main idea.

Horses have been used by mankind for a very long time. There is evidence to show they began to be caught and tamed around 6000 years ago. Many thousands of years before that, drawings of wild horses being hunted became part of cave art.

Now label each sentence **main idea** or **detail**:

Horses have been used by mankind for a very long time. _____

There is evidence to show they began to be caught and tamed around 6000 years ago. _____

Many thousands of years before that, drawings of wild horses being hunted became part of cave art. _____

Shetland ponies are famous for their size, strength and ability to put up with very harsh winters. They are very hardy. When there is no grass to eat, they will forage for seaweed along the shoreline.

Now label each sentence **main idea** or **detail**:

Shetland ponies are famous for their size, strength and ability to endure very harsh winters. _____

They are very hardy. _____

When there is no grass to eat, they will forage for seaweed along the shoreline. _____

## FLOWERING PLANTS

In the following paragraphs, one sentence is the **main idea**. The other sentences contain further **details** to support the main idea.

Flowering plants that rely on insects often have large, colourful flowers and a sweet scent. They all need to be pollinated somehow. Flowers that use the wind are usually dull brown or green.

Write out the sentence containing the main idea:

_____

A hummingbird has a long beak and even longer tongue. While it hovers over a flower for its nectar, sticky pollen grains stick to its beak. The bird then transfers the grains to the next flower. In this way, the bird pollinates flowers by accident.

The main idea is:

_____

No bats – no chocolate! Some plants round the world depend totally on bats for their pollination. Important examples include banana, mango and, of course, cocoa from which chocolate is made. Some bats have specially long tongues to reach nectar deep inside flowers. While bees and other insects are attracted to flowers that open during the day, bats rely on nocturnal flowers.

The main idea is:

_____

# THINK OF A TITLE

Read these short pieces of writing and circle the title that fits them best.

It is generally agreed that there are 7 continents: Africa, Antarctica, Asia, Australia, Europe, North America and South America. Islands located near a continent are usually thought of as being part of that continent.

| Continents of the World | Africa: the Biggest Continent | European Islands |

Mount Everest is the highest mountain in the world. It is over 29,035 feet or 8850 metres above sea level. If you were to include mountains that start below sea level, the highest would be Mauna Kea on Hawaii, which, from bottom to top, is 30,610 feet or 9330 metres.

| Mount Everest: the Facts | Mauna Kea: Record Breaker | High Mountains of the World |

There are different kinds of deserts, not just sandy ones. Experts agree that a desert is a place that gets less than 10 inches of rain in a year. That means that the Sahara is the largest hot desert, but the polar desert of Antarctica is even bigger.

| It's Hot in the Sahara | What is a Desert? | Antarctica is a Polar Desert |

The Nile in Africa is considered to be the longest river in the world. The Amazon in South America is the second longest, followed by the Yangtze in China and the Mississippi in North America.

| The Nile is in Africa | The World's Longest River | The World's Longest Rivers |

# WHO AM I?

Here are some descriptions.  Look for clues and key words that tell you who or what is being described.

I am big, with scales and fiery breath, and I love scaring people.

_____

I like hats, mostly pointed ones. Children are nice too – in soup!

_____

I am shiny with a sharp point. I belong to King Arthur.

_____

You can try to get in, but you'd have to climb a wall without falling into my moat.

_____

I know it's made of straw and it could be blown away, but I call it home.

_____

I might not be the best looking guy around, but why do I have to put up with goats on the roof?

_____

That boy isn't very bright.  Fancy swapping me for a bag of beans.

_____

I don't know why the bears were cross about the broken chair.

_____

# RED NOSE DAY

Read this about Red Nose Day. Then write down what each paragraph is about: its **main idea**. The catch is you're not allowed to write more than **20** words for each idea.

Red Nose Day, organised by Comic Relief, has become a special day all over Britain. Lots of people love to get involved. Every two years, up and down the country, in schools, businesses and local communities, people do something funny to raise money for charity.

_____

The BBC hosts a night of entertainment, involving all sorts of stars and celebrities from the worlds of music, comedy, drama and sport to inspire the nation to give generously.

_____

The money raised by Red Nose Day helps people living tough lives across the UK and Africa. Events raise awareness of poverty as well as raising a smile on millions of faces.

_____

One of the main aims of the charity is to give as many children as possible the chance to have an education. The number of children attending primary school in Africa has increased by over 60 million since 2000.

_____

## FAIRYTALE WORLDS

Take a look at these four pieces of writing. You might recognise what stories they come from. What is the **main idea** in each of these passages?

The Evil Queen possessed something unique: a magic mirror. Every morning, she would go to her magic mirror and say, "Mirror, mirror on the wall, who is the fairest of them all?" This always pleased the Queen, until one day she didn't get the answer she was hoping for.

_____

When Jack's mother tells him to take their one and only cow to market, she doesn't expect him to return with a bag of magic beans. She is so upset she throws them out of the window. But in the middle of the night those magic beans grow into a beanstalk that touches the clouds.

_____

Aladdin is ordered by his master, the wicked sorcerer, to climb down into the cave to fetch an oil lamp. It is no ordinary oil lamp, however. When Aladdin accidentally rubs it, a genie appears unexpectedly and offers to grant him anything he wishes for.

_____

Pinocchio's nose is not like any normal nose. When he lies to the fairy about losing his gold pieces, his nose grows longer. When he keeps on lying, his nose behaves in magical ways, growing so long Pinocchio can't get through the door.

_____

**There is something that is common to all of these passages. What is it?**

_____

# Summarising main ideas

Strand:    Comprehension

**National Curriculum reference:**

- identifying main ideas drawn from more than one paragraph and summarising these

**Reading Test / Content Domain links:**  2a, 2b, 2c, 2f

# PIRATES

Read this about pirates and draw lines to show what happened first, second and third (and fourth).

Anne Bonney disguised herself as a man and joined the crew of the well-known pirate, Captain Jack Rackham. His ship flew his famous skull and crossed daggers flag. Much of their time was spent attacking Spanish treasure ships.

| | |
|---|---|
| Anne joined Captain Jack Rackham | 1 |
| She attacked Spanish treasure ships | 2 |
| Anne disguised herself as a man | 3 |

Captain Hook is a character created by J. M. Barrie in 'Peter Pan'. Hook's pirate ship is called 'Jolly Roger'.

In the book, Captain Hook captures Wendy and challenges Peter to a duel. When Hook is beaten, Peter kicks him overboard to be eaten by the crocodile that has a ticking clock inside.

| | |
|---|---|
| Hook is kicked overboard | 1 |
| Hook challenges Peter to a duel | 2 |
| Hook captures Wendy | 3 |
| J. M. Barrie created Peter Pan | 4 |

## TAKING NOTE

Read these texts, then write down some **notes** (not sentences) describing the main ideas.

> ### Wildlife in Spring
>
> All of the 17 species of bats in the UK eat insects;  some as many as 3000 bugs in one night.
>
> Hedgehogs eat slugs, snails, beetles and earthworms.   Their babies are called hoglets.  Hoglets don't hunt for themselves until they are about 8 weeks old.

_____

_____

_____

> ### Big Schools' Birdwatch
>
> The Big Schools' Birdwatch has been running for more than ten years and helps to track the numbers of different birds in school grounds.   Nearly 90%  of schools that took part  reported  seeing more  blackbirds  than any other kind of bird.  An average of seven birds were spotted per school.
>
> Starlings  came second and, for the first time ever,  house sparrows came third.
>
> A record-breaking 90,000  pupils and their teachers counted birds for one hour in one day in the first half of Spring Term.

_____

_____

_____

# BLACKBEARD

Here is some information about the life of the pirate known as Blackbeard.
Once you've read it through, number the statements in the correct order.

Edward Teach was one of the most feared pirates of all time. He was called Blackbeard, because his large black beard covered most of his face. He was a large man, often carrying two swords, numerous knives, and pistols, and so was feared by his own crew.

He began his pirating career sometime after 1713, though he didn't at that time have his own ship. In the winter of 1717, Blackbeard began sailing the Caribbean with his own two ships. By attacking other vessels in the spring of 1718, Blackbeard soon took control of four pirate ships, as well as over 300 pirates.

In mid-1718 Blackbeard deliberately ran his ship, the *Queen Anne's Revenge*, onto a sand bank and destroyed it. His plan was to see Charles Eden, the Governor of North Carolina and ask for a pardon. For a while, Blackbeard lived there as a law-abiding citizen. But it didn't take him long to take up piracy again, this time, sharing any stolen goods with Charles Eden.

A fleet of Royal Navy ships surprised Blackbeard on November 22, 1718, when he was killed. As a pirate, Blackbeard captured over 40 ships. Although his life of crime lasted only a few years, his fearsome reputation has long outlived him.

☐ **It didn't take Blackbeard long to take up piracy again**

☐ **In 1717 Blackbeard began sailing with his own two ships**

☐ **Blackbeard began his pirating career after 1713**

☐ **The Royal Navy surprised Blackbeard**

☐ **Blackbeard ran his ship onto a sand bank**

# AN INDIAN TALE

In this story, based on traditional Indian tales, you need to know:

- **ragi** is a type of cereal
- **chowkabara** is a well-known Indian board game similar to Ludo.

Once you have read the first part of this story, answer the questions. Remember you can return to look for answers at any time.

## Babala the Giant – part 1

Sontash stopped farming for the day as a jungle crow flew overhead. "Oh, what must it be like," he thought, "to get a bird's eye view of my little farm?" He sighed and thought about his field of ragi, his six chickens, four pigs, three banana trees and one cow.

As he slept under the banyan tree, there was a BOOM like the rumble of thunder! Then another crashing THUMP! It sounded as if the grandfather of all elephants had just tripped over a squirrel.

As the sun rose, a boulder, bigger than a house, dropped from the sky. It landed ten fields away from Sontash's farm. It had been dropped by the giant called Babala – so tall his head touched the clouds. So tall that the black kites that soar high above were circling round his knees.

"Hey!" shouted Sontash, but the giant didn't notice him.

Priti, his wife, who always stuck by him, called to Sontash. "Climb to the top of the banyan tree. He might see you there."

He reached the top just as Babala dropped another huge boulder. It hit the ground just six fields away. What an ear-splitting noise it made. As if the moon had lost its way and bumped into the Earth.

"Hey! Babala!" shouted Sontash. "Why are you trying to destroy my field?"

"Field?" said Babala, bending down so low that his face drew close to Sontash. "What you call *field* is one of the squares of my board game. My chowkabara game. And these rocks are my chowkabara pieces. These logs are my dice. How dare you interrupt my game!"

1.   Who is the hero in this story?

     _____

2.   Who does the hero depend on, no matter what?

     _____

3.   Who is the villain?

     _____

4.   Do you think Sontash is rich or poor?

     _____

5.   What evidence is there for thinking he is rich or poor?

     _____

6.   What would he like to be able to do?

     _____

7.   What does the giant threaten to do to the farm?

     _____

     _____

8.   Imagine you have to tell this story to a friend.  Re-write it in your own words.
     The challenge is to include all the main points using no more than 50 words.

     _____

     _____

     _____

     _____

     _____

     _____

     _____

## Babala the Giant – part 2

Babala was about to roll his logs, destroying the farm, when Sontash yelled, "Wait! One person on their own can't play chowkabara. You need at least two people to play the game."

While the giant was thinking, Sontash quickly climbed down the banyan tree and immediately went to work to cut the field of ragi. But not all of it. All he cut was two lines joining the corners. Now the field had a cross in the middle.

Babala the giant looked down at Sontash's field. "Oh dear," he said. "I cannot land on a square with a cross."

"If you land on this field with a cross, you will lose your chowkabara pieces." Babala held the two logs in his hands. He rattled them around wildly. He blew on them for luck. Then he threw them onto the ground.

Sontash wasn't tall enough to count the number of dots on the sides of the logs. But all the giant said was, "Oh, no! Six." He sat down on a nearby hill looking glum. "You've won, Sontash, and I will leave all my chowkabara pieces on this little hill next to your farm. Goodbye."

"Thank you, Babala!" Sontash shouted.

The next evening, when all the farm work was done, Sontash and Priti climbed to the top of the enormous boulders that Babala had left. And together, just like the jungle crow, they were able to see all of their farm – the field of ragi, the six chickens, the four pigs and the three banana trees and the cow.

1. Do you think Babala wants to destroy the farm?  Why do you think this?

   _____

   _____

2. What two things does Sontash do to outwit the giant?

   _____

   _____

3. What does the story tell you about the rules of chowkabara?

   _____

   _____

4. This story has a happy ending.  Describe it.

   _____

   _____

   _____

5. Now try to re-tell this part of the story in less than 50 words.

   _____

   _____

   _____

   _____

   _____

   _____

   _____

## Details that support the main idea

**Strand:**     Comprehension

**National Curriculum reference:**

- identifying main ideas drawn from more than one paragraph and summarising these

**Reading Test / Content Domain links:**   2a, 2b, 2c, 2f

# BIRDS OF A FEATHER

Here are some **main ideas** about birds.  Find the **detail** that goes with each of them.  One has been done for you.

| | |
|---|---|
| Some owls are easier to spot than others. | You can do bird-spotting from your kitchen window. |
| The kingfisher's blue wings make it one of our most colourful birds. | The Barn Owl has white feathers under its wings and body. |
| The robin is easy to spot in your garden. | Its feathers come in amazing colours. |
| The starling, though still quite common, is in decline. | Populations of the distinctive yellow bird have 'dropped like a stone'. |
| The skylark is often heard before it is seen. | Recently, numbers have gone down by around 70%. |
| Swallows migrate to Britain in early summer to have their young. | Despite its striking colours many gardeners would prefer it to stay away. |
| The wren is a small, brown, well-camouflaged bird, with a sharp, trilling song. | It's not so easy to spot, but, once you know its song, you'll know when it's nearby. |
| Yellowhammer numbers have halved in the last twenty years. | Its clear, high melodic song can last for five minutes or even longer. |
| The red and black bullfinch often visits gardens, feeding on the buds of fruit trees. | They often return to the same nesting site year after year. |

## HEROES AND VILLAINS

Here are descriptions of heroes and villains.  How do you know which is which?
Pick out a word or phrase from the text that tells you.

# Heroes

# Villains

George's lance was broken but he took
out his sword and fought on bravely.

The dragon appeared to be about to fly
off when it turned on him viciously.

_____

_____

Arthur was young, with no experience,
but everyone knew he could be trusted.

A secret smile crossed the wizard's lips
as he left to work on his next evil spell.

_____

_____

Perhaps Jack wasn't the brightest child
in the village but he didn't scare easily.

Everyone in the village was terrified at
the sound of the approaching giant.

_____

_____

The woodcutter risked his own life by
setting the two children free.

No one told Hansel and Gretel about the
strange owner of the house of sweets.

_____

_____

The Prince was determined to find the
girl lost in the enchanted forest.

The Queen took her magic mirror off
the wall and smashed it on the floor.

_____

_____

## SCHOOL SPORTS

Here is some information about Uptown School's sports day. From the three possibilities, tick **one detail** that supports each **main idea**.

> Alice and Marta won the 3-legged race.

They edged in front when Carla and Fatima fell near the winning line. _____

Mrs Williams from Class 3 fired the starting pistol. _____

Nearly everybody's parents turned up to watch. _____

> The toddlers' potato and spoon race was funny.

The potatoes were supplied by Mr Green the grocer. _____

Some children held their potato in one hand and the spoon in the other. _____

We were lucky to have fine weather for the events. _____

> Tomasz in Class 4 surprised everyone by winning the skipping race.

He was wearing white shorts and a black t-shirt. _____

His older brother, Patryk, came second in the 100 metres. _____

He started slowly but came rapidly from behind. _____

> Each class was split fairly into different teams and named after animals.

There are six classes in Uptown School. _____

Mr Carter made sure that each team had the same number of children. _____

Mr Carter's daughter, Anna, has just started school. _____

## ONCE UPON A TIME

Everybody knows that Little Red Riding Hood was kind and that the Big Bad Wolf was big and bad. Find the words and phrases in this introduction that tell you what the two characters were like and write them inside the boxes.

"Mother," said Little Red Riding Hood, baking some cakes, "I'm going to take these to Granny." Her mother agreed, but warned her not to talk to any strangers on her way through the forest.

As Little Red Riding Hood skipped along, taking care not to squash any tiny creatures on the path, she decided to pick some flowers to brighten up the old woman's cottage.

Creeping out from some dark bushes, Mr Wolf appeared in front of her. Hiding a snarl behind a fake smile, he asked Little Red Riding Hood where she was going.

Always polite, she explained she was off to see her grandmother in the thatched cottage by the brook. Mr Wolf wished her a safe journey, but had a sly chuckle to himself as he ran off. He knew a shortcut that would take him to the old woman's cottage before Little Red Riding Hood. What a sneak!

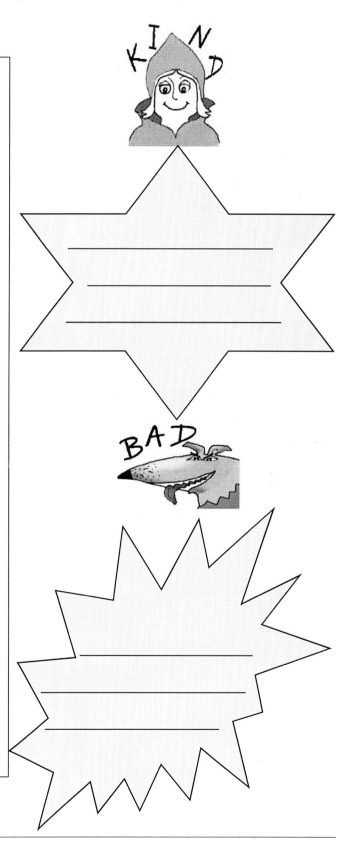

# THE GOLDEN EAGLE

Here is an information leaflet about the Golden Eagle.  What is it mainly about?

### The Golden Eagle

In Britain, Golden Eagles are to be found mainly in the Highlands of Scotland and Cumbria.

With their large, hooked beaks and excellent eyesight, they are powerful predators.  Using their strong talons and remarkable wingspan,  they can easily spot and swoop down on their prey.

Mainly, they eat other birds and small mammals, but they have been blamed by angry farmers for taking new-born lambs.

What is the leaflet mainly about?  Tick the correct one.

**The Scottish Highlands**

**The Golden Eagle is a predator**

**Farmers are angry**

Write a sentence from the leaflet that helped you to make your choice:

_____

_____

# BATS

Here is a page from a reference book about bats. There are all sorts of information that could be written about bats. What is the main thing this page is about?

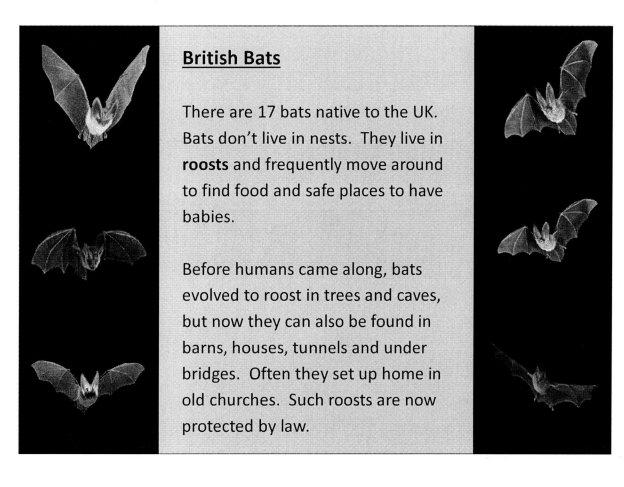

## British Bats

There are 17 bats native to the UK. Bats don't live in nests. They live in **roosts** and frequently move around to find food and safe places to have babies.

Before humans came along, bats evolved to roost in trees and caves, but now they can also be found in barns, houses, tunnels and under bridges. Often they set up home in old churches. Such roosts are now protected by law.

What is the **main idea** in this text? Tick the correct box:

How bats have evolved ◯

Old churches in Britain ◯

Where bats live ◯

Make a note of 2 things that helped you make your choice:

| | |
|---|---|
| | |

## SCHOOL FÊTE

Here is a message for parents and carers that has been put on the school website concerning the school fête.

**DRIZZLETOWN PRIMARY SCHOOL, LOWER WETBURY, WILTS**

### School Fête – Saturday 1st July

Every year, as you all know, Drizzletown Primary School holds its annual fête on the school playing field. Unfortunately, because of the flooding that has taken place, this year's fête has had to be cancelled. Letters have been sent home, but in case these have been overlooked, I would appreciate it if you passed on this information to your friends. We hope to avoid last year's situation when so many visitors got lost in the fog. I'm sure, as parents, you are as disappointed as I am by this last-minute decision, but, as a result of the recent torrential rain, cancellation is inevitable.

Mr. I. M. Drenched (Headteacher)

What is the main idea in this online message? Tick the correct box.

the fête is held on the playing field ◯

letters have been sent home ◯

the fête is cancelled ◯

people will be disappointed ◯

Make a note of 3 things that helped you make your choice.

|  |  |  |
|---|---|---|
|  |  |  |

# Inferences

Strand:    Making inferences

National Curriculum reference:

- drawing inferences such as inferring characters' feelings, thoughts and motives from their actions

Reading Test / Content Domain links:   2a, 2b, 2d, 2f, 2g

## WHAT'S MY JOB?

Using the clues available in the way these people describe their jobs, work out what they do.

I work in forests and need an axe. I am a _____

If you visit me, I'll check your pulse. I am a _____

It takes a while to mark all the homework. I am a _____

I ring your doorbell and give you a letter. I am a _____

Don't break the speed limit. I am a _____

I'll let you know about tomorrow's weather. I am a _____

Pulling this tooth out won't hurt a bit. I am a _____

If your tap is leaking, I'll come and fix it. I am a _____

I can see the planet Earth through my window. I am an _____

Soon, you'll see out of the window more easily. I am a _____

That will be £2.50, please. Would you like a bag? I am a _____

I'll be able to stop once this corn is cut. I am a _____

It took me six months to finish this portrait. I am an _____

# DETECTIVE WORK

Look for the clues in this text and work on the answers:

**Sam checked the calendar. "Tomorrow," she said, "it will be Monday 24th – my birthday. Hooray!" She clapped her hands. Opening the curtains, she grumbled. "I do hope the weather improves by then."**

1.      Is Sam a girl or a boy?    _____

2.      How do you know?    _____

3.      What day is it?          _____

4.      How does Sam feel before the curtains are opened?    _____

_____

5.      How can you tell how Sam feels?    _____

_____

6.      How does Sam feel after the curtains are opened?    _____

_____

7.      What word tells you how Sam felt then?    _____

8.      What do you think the weather was like outside?    _____

_____

## WHAT ARE THEY UP TO?

The way characters speak – for example, whether they shout or whisper – can give us clues about what they are like, how they are feeling and what they are up to. What do you think these characters might be doing?

| how they spoke | what are they doing? |
|---|---|
| The giant roared. | |
| The children whispered. | |
| The knight yelled. | |
| The messenger reported. | |
| The teacher snapped. | |
| The detective questioned. | |
| The customer complained. | |
| The school janitor grumbled. | |
| The princess screamed. | |
| The Queen announced. | |
| The prisoner moaned. | |
| The baby cried. | |

# I KNOW HOW YOU FEEL

Every day we have to work out how people are feeling from the look on their face, how they are standing, the way they speak and their actions. We can work out that a friend is sad without them saying they feel sad. This is a clever skill called **inference**.

Underline the evidence and describe how these children feel.

Roberto stamped his foot and waved his hands in the air. He walked away from the referee, stared up at the sky and shook his head. He turned to the crowd and shrugged his shoulders.

**feelings:**

_____

**feelings:**

_____

Tess opened the envelope, careful not to damage the letter inside. She felt her pulse racing as she slowly unfolded the blue notepaper. She couldn't believe it, but it was true. She had won!

Raj sighed deeply, threw his pencil onto the floor and leaned back in his chair. He looked at the page of homework again, but it was no use. He turned back to the instructions but that didn't help.

**feelings:**

_____

**feelings:**

_____

Luisa turned her back on the group of friends. The corners of her mouth drooped and she had to hold back the tears. Taking one last look back at her so-called friends, she shuffled off.

© Copyright HeadStart Primary Ltd

# EYE-WITNESSES

Several people witnessed the same scene: a man drove off in a car. But the witnesses had different information. Using what they tell you, decide what was happening.

## What's happening here?

I saw him check his watch and jump in the car. He drove like the wind.

_____

_____

_____

That car must have been left unlocked. He didn't use a key. Off he went.

_____

_____

_____

The car was parked right outside the bank. He had a bag. He was in a hurry.

_____

_____

_____

I'm sure he had a camera with him. The Queen was visiting the local school.

_____

_____

_____

His daughter was in the back of the car. Looked very ill, if you ask me.

_____

_____

_____

So, in the end, using all the evidence, what do you think happened?

_____

# Justifying inferences with evidence

**Strand:**   Making inferences

**National Curriculum reference:**

- drawing inferences such as inferring characters' feelings, thoughts and motives from their actions, and justifying inferences with evidence

**Reading Test / Content Domain links:**   2a, 2b, 2d, 2f, 2g

# CHARACTERS IN THEIR OWN WORDS

One way of working out what somebody in a book is like is by reading what they say. This is useful because it gives you some idea of how they might behave in certain situations. For instance, they might stand and fight, run away or try to sort things out. Here is a list of characters and a list of characteristics (what they are like). Can you draw lines to match them up?

I want my porridge and I don't want to see anybody sitting on my chair. Got that?

shy

I don't understand how anybody can be bothered to make porridge. I'd prefer to stay in bed all day.

brave

I don't mind sharing my porridge with Goldilocks. She can sit on my chair for a while too.

bossy

Dragon? You show me this dragon. I'll teach it to wander around scaring all the villagers.

kind

All I'm trying to do is to get out a bit more instead of hiding away in my cave all day.

lazy

**Now record your answers on the next page.**

## NOW WHAT ARE THEY GOING TO DO?

Write your answers from the previous page under the characters.   Then write down how you think they might behave.

## WHAT ARE THEY LIKE?

Read this introduction to a mystery story.  The four children in it are all different.
When the strange thing happens, what do you think they will say and do?

You could tell from the look on Charlie's face that he'd had enough.  He'd already told us all that he thought having a midnight feast in Cora's back garden was a stupid idea.  Why he turned up none of us knew.  He spent all night pretending to yawn.  Cora had done really well.  The food was delicious.  If it was her hope to overcome her shyness and make new friends, then she had done an excellent job.  Pity about Rita.  Always telling the rest of us what to do.  Me?  I'll be friends with anybody. People say to me: 'Joey, nothing and nobody ever gets you down.  You put up with everybody and face up to everything life throws at you.'  I guess it's true.  Funny how things turned out.  Nobody thought we'd be the only kids on the entire planet to witness the high-pitched screeching, the space around us filling with thick, green mist and the ground shaking underneath us.  As the air cleared, we found ourselves staring at a round metal ball the size of a truck.
And... it was opening...

| name | what do they say? | what do they do? |
|---|---|---|
| Charlie | | |
| Cora | | |
| Rita | | |
| Joey | | |

# PANDORA JONES AND THE BIRTHDAY BOX

Here is a boxful of words that describe feelings. They might help you to work out what Pandora Jones is feeling at each stage of this short story.

| annoyed | pleased | thrilled | surprised | frustrated |
| scared | nervous | miserable | relieved |

Underline the evidence that tells you how she might be feeling and choose a word that describes it.

| story | feelings |
|---|---|
| Checking that no one was watching her, Pandora Jones slowly turned the door handle. As her eyes opened wide, she put her hand over her mouth to stifle a squeal. | |
| Tomorrow was her birthday, not today. Checking again over her shoulder, as quietly as possible, she took a step toward the huge box tied with ribbon. Her heart pounded. | |
| She tugged and twisted the ribbon, but, no matter how hard she tried, it wouldn't undo. Using all her strength, she did her best to rip it apart. This was getting her nowhere. | |
| Then she remembered the scissors that were kept in a drawer. In no time, the ribbon lay in shreds on the floor. At last, she sighed deeply as she removed the lid. | |
| Strangely, the box seemed to be empty. Why would anybody go to all that trouble with an empty box? Then, in a corner of the box, she spotted a note from her brother. On it was scribbled one word: NAUGHTY! | |

© Copyright HeadStart Primary Ltd

# Predicting what might happen

Strand:     Making inferences

**National Curriculum reference:**

- predicting what might happen from details stated and implied

**Reading Test / Content Domain links:**   2a, 2b, 2g

## AND THEN...

Using the clues, what are these people about to do?

1.     The girl pushed the chocolate flake into the tub of ice cream.

_____

2.     When the man put on his coat, the dog got up and sat by the door.

_____

3.     Mum and Dad parked in the car park and took out the shopping bags.

_____

4.     Grandma looked at the sky and took her umbrella out of her bag.

_____

5.     The decorator propped his ladder next to the window and carried up his paint.

_____

6.     Once the suitcases and maps were in the car, we drove off.

_____

7.     Grandad made us stand still and fetched his camera.

_____

8.     Gathering up eleven pairs of dirty shorts, I took out the washing powder.

_____

9.     We all lined up and waited for the sound of the starting pistol.

_____

10.    Holding the bunch of flowers behind my back, I rang my neighbour's doorbell.

_____

## WHAT HAPPENED NEXT?

You can't always predict if something good or bad is about to happen.  Some actions are riskier than others.  Write down what you think might happen.

Jenna walks out of the room carrying six plates, five cups and a milk jug.

GOOD

_____

_____

BAD

_____

_____

Harry gets ready as big Barry comes running at him with the rugby ball.

GOOD

_____

_____

BAD

_____

_____

Looking for the exit, the school visitor walks into the cleaning cupboard.

GOOD

_____

_____

BAD

_____

_____

My aunts and uncles are having tea when a mouse pops out of the cake.

GOOD

_____

_____

BAD

_____

_____

## WHERE DO WE GO FROM HERE?

Use your detective skills to check for clues about what is going on and how the characters might behave. Then write more of their stories.

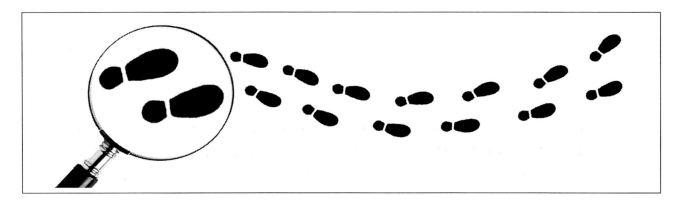

1.    The rabbits were feeding happily in the field until . . .

    _____

2.    Day after day, the cheese forgotten in the fridge got smellier until . . .

    _____

3.    Ben watched the cricketers from his hospital window. "If only . . .

    _____

    _____

4.    As soon as Ahmed filled the bird feeder . . .

    _____

    _____

5.    After training for months, Pattie knew this was going to be her big moment. Carefully, she placed the ball on the penalty spot and stared hard at the goalkeeper.

    _____

    _____

    _____

6.   Up to that moment, Rajeev was sure he was alone in the house. Then something crunched under his foot. He stared at the trail of cake crumbs on the floor. It could mean only one thing.

_____

_____

_____

7.   Soo Lin suddenly woke, relieved that it had all been a dream. So when the doorbell rang and she looked out of the window, she expected to see her friends waiting. What a shock she got, when there, at her front door was . . .

_____

_____

_____

8.   Jordan felt a little nervous at the start of the mountain bike race. It wasn't simply that he was up against some hard-riding rivals. He knew he was one of the best of them. No, it was more to do with the route. These hills and forests of eastern Europe were still the home of wolves and bears. Not to mention creatures who came out only at night.

_____

_____

_____

_____

_____

_____

# Features of texts

Strand:     Comprehension / Themes and Conventions

**National Curriculum reference:**

- identifying how language, structure and presentation contribute to meaning
- identifying themes and conventions in a wide range of books

**Reading Test / Content Domain links:**   2a, 2b, 2f, 2g

## ON THE BOOK SHELVES

Here are some features of different types of writing. Draw lines linking the features to the book or pages you'd find them in. One has been done for you.

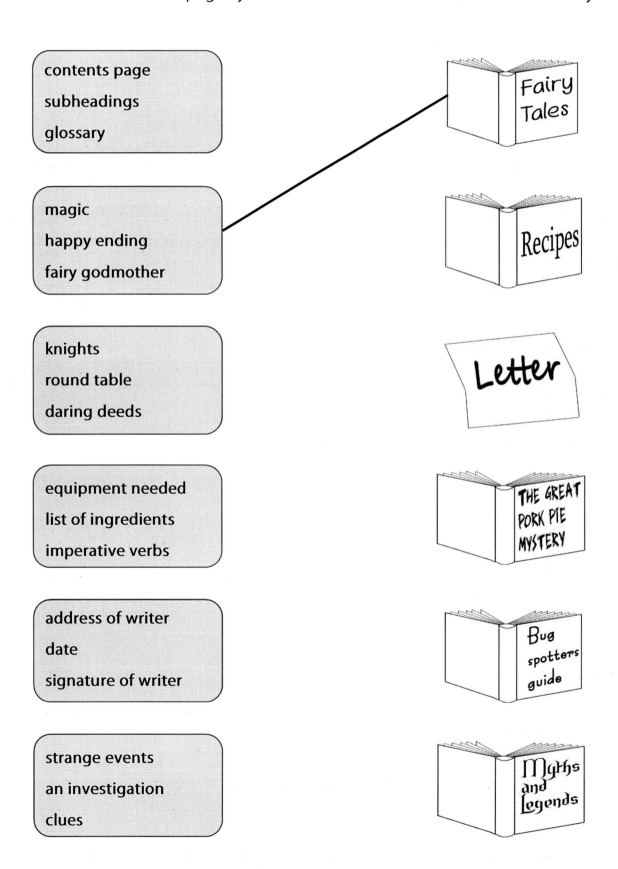

contents page

subheadings

glossary

Fairy Tales

magic

happy ending

fairy godmother

Recipes

knights

round table

daring deeds

Letter

equipment needed

list of ingredients

imperative verbs

THE GREAT PORK PIE MYSTERY

address of writer

date

signature of writer

Bug spotters guide

strange events

an investigation

clues

Myths and Legends

© Copyright HeadStart Primary Ltd

# MORE WRITING STYLES

Now look at these short pieces of writing and decide whether they are part of :

- information text
- instructions
- myths and legends
- mystery stories
- fairytales
- letters

| | | |
|---|---|---|
| Cut carefully round the reindeer shape before attaching the string. | I look forward to hearing from you soon. Best wishes, | King Arthur stood in front of his knights, a grim look on his face. |
| _____ | _____ | _____ |
| Dear Sir, I would like to complain about recycling. | Then Prince Handsome picked up the glass slipper, but she'd gone. | As far as Maggie could see, the Inspector was completely clueless. |
| _____ | _____ | _____ |
| The greatest threat to our native species is the Harlequin Ladybird. | thunder...........p 9, 22, 87 tornadoes.......p 7, 12, 65 typhoons....... p 3, 41, 99 | There seemed to be nothing magical about the beans.  "Oh, Jack!" |
| _____ | _____ | _____ |
| Karl looked in despair at the empty box. The jewels were gone! | Wet your finger and hold it up in the air.  Check to see which side has dried. | The labyrinth was deep and echoed with the Minotaur's groans. |
| _____ | _____ | _____ |

# TRADITIONAL GAMES

This page is all about traditional games played by children. Decide whether the text is written in the style of a piece of information, instructions, a diary entry, or a mystery story. Give your reasons.

Saturday.

Today I played hide and seek in the park with my friends. We were having a picnic when it started to rain.

_____

_____

_____

_____

_____

Marie emptied her bag of chestnuts on the grass, all ready for a game of conkers. But one was making a strange ringing sound.

_____

_____

_____

_____

To play Hot Potato, you need a ball or a beanbag, at least six children and someone to act as caller. Stand in a circle. Choose someone to start.

_____

_____

_____

_____

In Victorian times, it was common for children to play in the street. Long before the invention of computer games, children played hopscotch ...

_____

_____

_____

_____

## ON THE OTHER HAND

When we compare two different sports, pets, shops, bicycles or anything else, certain key words and phrases, such as **both, the same as, different from**, as well as others, make it clear what is similar and different about the two things.  Underline those key words and phrases in the following texts.

Sometimes, Mum makes her own pizzas. They're different from take-away pizzas, although both are tasty.  On the one hand, Mum's have fresh tomatoes, while the ones we buy from PizzaPup don't.  What they have in common is me ready to eat them.

My friend, Charlie, has a cat, but I have a dog. I'd always have a dog instead of a cat.  Both make excellent pets, but, unlike cats, dogs can learn to do what you tell them.  The opposite is true for cats.  They wander about doing what they feel like.  Charlie says he likes that about them.  That would drive me mad.

*While the Pound In Your Pocket shop sells everything at £1, our local supermarket, on the other hand, has a bigger range of things to buy.  Its size is similar to the supermarket, even though it doesn't display so much stuff on the shelves.  Although Pound In Your Pocket is a lot cheaper, the supermarket is better quality.*

While moths and butterflies both have six legs and powdery scales on their wings, usually, butterflies can be seen during the day, whereas, moths tend to come out at night. Unlike butterflies, moths don't have tiny club shapes on the end of their antennae. Another obvious difference is that butterflies are usually very colourful. The same cannot be said for moths, which are much duller. When they are resting, moths hold their wings flat. Butterflies, however, hold their wings together above the body.

# DANGEROUS ADVENTURE

Here is the beginning of an adventure story.  Highlight important features and say what they are.  These might include:

- adjectives and similes **describing** places and people
- **dramatic events** sometimes written in short, snappy sentences
- **risky situations** and characters in **danger**
- important **task** that must be done, such as a **rescue**
- **catchy title**

_____

_____

_____

_____

_____

_____

_____

_____

_____

_____

_____

## Follow the Leader

The moonlight suddenly disappeared as if someone had thrown a blanket over it.  Aziz and Naomi glanced at each other, wondering if this was such a good idea after all.

Follow the leader.  It was Joe's idea.  But he hadn't mentioned climbing the high fence into the scrap yard: a cemetery for the cool, dream cars of American movies.  Mustangs, Impalas, Chevrolets, Thunderbirds.  All here,  piled up  high  and Joe's particular dream sat on top of six other wrecks.

'No way,' whispered Aziz.  'No one is going to climb up there.'

'Chicken?' said Joe, wiping his oily hands on his ragged hoodie before stepping  onto  the  bent bumper of the first car.  He was half-way up when Naomi froze.  There  was  a  creak.  A  groaning  of rusting  metal. And  the  red  Mustang balanced on top of the tower of cars started to sway.

_____

_____

_____

_____

_____

_____

_____

_____

_____

_____

_____

# CLOWNING AROUND

What kind of text is this?  Highlight and describe its features and make your decision.

---

**The Art of Clowning** by J. Grimaldi

Chapters:

1. History    p. 5
2. Skills     p. 72
Glossary      p. 126

### Chapter 1    **History**

Research shows that clowns were there in Greek and Roman times.  Throughout the Middle Ages, kings, queens and nobles had their fools and jesters, who had a good life as long as they amused their masters...

### Chapter 2    **Skills**

Clowning is not as easy as it looks, requiring many physical skills, acting abilities, imagination and wit.  It uses timing, surprise and slapstick.  Clowns have their own special tricks and surprise elements, e.g. flowers that squirt water and custard pies...

### Glossary

**slapstick:**  1.  action comedy. e.g. throwing pies in actors' faces.
2.  stick, making a loud slap, used by clowns for striking other performers.

---

This text is: _____

© Copyright HeadStart Primary Ltd

# Features of texts and meaning

Strand:     Comprehension / Themes and Conventions

National Curriculum reference:

- identifying how language, structure and presentation contribute to meaning
- recognising some different forms of poetry
- identifying themes and conventions in a wide range of books

Reading Test / Content Domain links:   2a, 2b, 2f, 2g

## FUN WITH SHAPES

Why has the writer written these words and sentences like this?

I'M NOT scared at all — eeeek

_____

_____

I don't enjoy cycling along this bumpy road

_____

_____

DON'T WALK TOO CLOSE TO THE EDGE OF THE

C

_____ L

_____ I . . .

DRIVING TOO FAST CAN

LEAD TO .    .    .    .    .   . . . . //!

_____

_____

## SHAPE POEM

Here is a shape poem (or calligram).

1.  Why do you think the writer arranged the words like this?

    _____

    _____


2.  What other shapes might the writer have used?

    _____


3.  What words might the writer have used with a bird shape?

    _____

    _____

# MYSTERY AND ADVENTURE

Here are some paragraphs taken from mystery and adventure stories. When you read them, it's worth spotting the key words.

Ever since Jake was five years old, he had wanted to be a detective. It was no surprise that the rest of his family got pretty fed up of him spying on them all the time.

Detectives, of course, must be good at spotting clues, noticing unusual things happening, such as Grandad going to the loo and not coming back.

1.      How has the author made a link between the two paragraphs?

_____

_____

_____

From her bedroom window, Nicola could see beyond the village to the hills and the outlines of oaks. But tonight, there was something else. Something strange. A light streaking across the sky. Not a shooting star. No. Something else.

People had talked about lights in the sky before, but they were cranks. Wacky. Imagining things. But now here they were.

2.      How do you know that these two paragraphs are part of the same story?

_____

_____

_____

## PLAY TIME

Here is part of a play.  It is set out to help the audience understand who the characters are, what is going on and where it is happening.  It's also written to help the actors know how to act.   In a playscript, you will find:

- a title
- cast list (the characters in the play)
- names of characters taking turns to speak
- description of the setting (where the action happens)
- stage directions
- speech (dialogue)

---

**The Party**

Cast: Aunt Rosie,  Max,  Kim

**Scene 1**

*The kitchen of Aunt Rosie's house.*

Aunt Rosie:   *(enters smiling)*  Max, help me make some cheese sandwiches for the

               party.

Kim:          That might not be a good idea.

Aunt Rosie:   *(puzzled)*  Why not?  Your friends will be here in an hour.

Kim:          Tell her, Max.

Max:          *(looking guilty)*  You tell her.

Kim:          *(shaking her head)*  Max ate all the cheese.  He's crazy about cheese.

               Don't ask me why.

Aunt Rosie:   Well, let's get the glasses and pour out some cola.

*Kim's face turns red as Max puts his hand on her shoulder.*

Aunt Rosie:   Oh dear!

---

1.    What is the title of the play?

_____

2.  Who are the characters in the play?

    _____

3.  Where does the action take place?

    _____

4.  Write down an example of stage directions.

    _____

5.  How do you know Aunt Rosie is cheerful when she first enters?

    _____

6.  Why is she puzzled?

    _____

    _____

7.  How does Max feel when Kim asks him to explain the missing cheese?

    _____

8.  What does Kim do while explaining to Aunt Rosie what has happened?

    _____

9.  Why do you think the writer of the play wrote: **Kim's face turns red as Max puts his hand on her shoulder**?

    _____

    _____

10. Can you suggest another title for the play?

    _____

11. Write a stage direction for Aunt Rosie when she says: **Oh dear!**

    _____

## LIFE CYCLES

Here are two descriptions of life cycles. To show the order in which they happen, the writer has used words such as **next**. Make a list of these key words.

There are four separate stages in the life cycle of a butterfly. Firstly, the female butterfly attaches its eggs to the underside of a leaf. The next stage is when the caterpillar emerges. While feeding on the leaf, it grows. As it gets bigger, it sheds its old skin several times. Then comes the chrysalis.

This is the third stage. Inside its cocoon, the caterpillar undergoes dramatic changes until a new adult butterfly crawls out to stretch and dry its wings. Finally, this adult is able to mate and reproduce.

_____

_____

_____

_____

_____

_____

The life cycle of a frog begins when an adult female lays its eggs in water. This is called spawn. Each egg starts life as a single cell. If the spawn isn't eaten by a fish or a duck, the cell splits into two, then four, until the egg is made up of lots of cells. This stage is called the embryo. This is when gills start to form.

After about 3 weeks, the embryo leaves its jelly-like egg and attaches itself to an underwater leaf. Once it is big enough, it becomes a tadpole with a long tail. After 5 weeks, it begins to change. First of all, hind legs appear. Next: front legs. Then the tail becomes smaller and lungs form inside. This is when you see them swimming to the surface to breathe in air.

Eleven or twelve weeks after the egg was part of a clump of spawn, a tiny frog leaves the pond and starts to eat worms and insects. Later, it will find a mate and the whole cycle will start all over again.

_____

_____

_____

_____

_____

_____

_____

_____

_____

_____

_____

© Copyright HeadStart Primary Ltd

# Words that capture the reader's imagination

Strand:     Language for effect

National Curriculum reference:

- discussing words and phrases that capture the reader's interest and imagination

Reading Test / Content Domain links:   2a, 2b, 2g

# SOUND WORDS

An **onomatopoeia** imitates the sound it is describing, such as the **bang** of a drum or the **meow** of a cat. Using the words in the box, fill in the gaps in the texts.

| coughing | beeping | humming | jingling | creaking | clapping |
|---|---|---|---|---|---|

### THE PERFORMANCE

The members of the  orchestra  played as well as they could.  The evening  could have been better if the audience had been a  bit  quieter.  Many of them were _____ at the wrong  time. We had  hardly  begun  when  several  phones started _____.  There was a constant _____ of  chairs.  Someone was having a _____ fit in the middle of the trumpet  solo.  I'm sure I could hear the annoying _____ of keys.  And it's nice to think people are keen to join in, but _____ out of tune doesn't help.

| giggling | sizzle | pitter-pattering | moan | clattering |
|---|---|---|---|---|
| chucking | squelched | splashing | whoop | drenched |

### WET DAY AT SCHOOL

The rain wasn't just making a pleasant _____ sound. No. It was _____ down as if some of those ancient Greek gods we've been studying were _____ it at us and _____.  I got _____ on the way home _____ through the puddles and _____ in the kitchen door.  I was about to _____ about the terrible day I'd had.  That's when I heard the _____ of sausages in the frying pan.  All I could do then was _____ with delight.

# MORE SOUNDS

Circle the examples of onomatopoeia in the following pieces of writing.

Hester clicked off the light switch, stepped outside and crunched along the gravel path. The gate squeaked as she pushed it open. The stars were out and a barn owl hooted among the rustling trees.

Jed admitted he was a bit clumsy at times. Not only that, I knew he was hungry the way his stomach grumbled. So I wasn't in the least surprised when he scuffled past me to the kitchen. The bottle of cola he was holding fizzed and splattered his t-shirt just as his huge plateful of snacks clattered across the kitchen floor. When he got hiccups I have to admit I couldn't stop myself howling with laughter.

I was happily strumming my guitar when I heard a screech of brakes outside my window. This was followed by the honking of a car horn. I've no idea what it was all about. The engine revved up again and, immediately, the car roared off. Seconds later, I heard the wail of a siren getting louder and louder until the police whizzed by in hot pursuit.

The cat was purring so I knew it was enjoying lapping up its milk. The dog, of course, wouldn't stop yapping even though it had munched up its dinner only minutes before. Since the cat wouldn't allow it to have any milk, it trudged outside and slurped some of the water from its bowl.

# EXAMPLES OF EXAGGERATION

To exaggerate means to describe something as being bigger, smaller, harder, easier, better or worse than it really is.  It can be effective.  It can be funny.  Fill in the table with your own examples of exaggeration as well as the same sentence without exaggeration.  One has already been done.

| exaggeration | without exaggeration |
|---|---|
| My feet are so big they're like boats. | I have big feet. |
| The fish I caught this morning was the size of a shark. | |
| I'm so hungry I could eat a horse. | |
| I'll die if Dad doesn't buy me that new computer game. | |
| You can't get in Harry's room for all his Marvel comics. | |
| | Mum will be angry when she finds out I ate all the sweets. |
| | I'm not very good at maths. |
| These shoes are killing me. | |
| | It's very cold today. |
| Sometimes my friends drive me up the wall. | |

# PAINTING PICTURES WITH WORDS

When we are describing something to somebody, we all use describing words. These are called **adjectives**. If, for example, a writer wants to create an even better picture in your head, he/she might compare it to something you know is similar. This is called a **simile**. It often creates a better picture than an adjective on its own.

**as tall as a skyscraper**

**like a speeding bullet**

Underline the **similes** in the following sentences and say how they make you think or feel.

1.  The sleeping baby looked as snug as a bug in a rug.

    _____

2.  When he had finished tidying, his bedroom was as clean as a whistle.

    _____

3.  Now that you've explained what happened, it's all as clear as mud.

    _____

4.  If you're active all day, you will sleep like a log.

    _____

5.  She was chosen for the school concert because she could sing like an angel.

    _____

6.  The trouble with inviting the giant for lunch is he eats like a pig.

    _____

7.  At the start of the summer holidays, I felt as free as a bird.

    _____

## SIMILAR SIMILES

Here is a poem made up of similes.  There are 12 altogether.  See how many you can find and record them below.  Remember they begin with 'like' or 'as'.

# THESEUS, BEWARE!

As big as a bulldozer, Minotaur stands.
Take care you're not caught by its dinner-plate hands.
The Minotaur's hair is as rough as a brush.
Intruder, watch out, you're turning to mush.
Running's no good, he's as fast as a fox
With muscles as huge as grandfather clocks.
Wide as the ocean, his mouth is so monstrous
Get close and his breath will knock you unconscious
Tail like a bullwhip cutting the air.
Eyes that see everything – Theseus, beware!

As black as pitch from the Earth's deepest mine,
This maze is amazing – it's labyrinthine!
You'll be lost as a grain of sand on a beach.
Don't cry for help, for help's out of reach.
You're as mad as a rabbit dazed by a headlight
But the Minotaur loves subterranean midnight.
He'll find you as sure as night follows day.
Look behind you!  A shadow is creeping this way.
Eyes like an eagle and claws like a snare.
Sword ready, Theseus?  Better beware!

|  |  |  |
| --- | --- | --- |
|  |  |  |
|  |  |  |
|  |  |  |
|  |  |  |

# LETTERS AND EMAILS

Here is a letter to a TV weather forecaster:

Dear Sir or Madam,

I would like to complain about the weather last Saturday. Arriving at the gates of Buckingham Palace at the crack of dawn, I was totally prepared to suffer sore feet and back-ache in order to catch a glimpse of the Queen. I did not expect to be bombarded by rain at midday and then to be blinded by sunshine at the very moment Her Majesty made her appearance.

I hope you will try to do a little better next weekend as I have tickets for an open-air rock concert.

Yours sincerely,

Gerald G. Grumpsville

Mr. Grumpsville chose his words carefully. Look at the words below in **bold**. Why do you think he used them? What effect do they have?

| words used | effect |
|---|---|
| Arriving at the gates of Buckingham Palace **at the crack of dawn** | |
| **bombarded** by rain... **blinded** by sunshine | |
| I hope you will **try to do a little better** next weekend | |

Mr Grumpsville took his children, Sally and Joe, to the rock concert. These are their emails to friends.

Hey Angie,

You're gonna be like green with envy 'cos guess where I went on Saturday? Dad took us to see our favourite band. Yeah! They were so cool. Later he bought us the monster of all monster pizzas. Pity Joe had to come too.

See ya – Sal  x

Hi Nick,

You missed a good one at the weekend. The music was the best. Pizzas too. Sally is like a kinda Scrooge. She could easily have given you her ticket. You should have seen her wolfing down the pizza. Gross!

Joe

Some of the words below are in **bold**. Why do you think the children chose them?

| words used | effect |
|---|---|
| You're gonna be like **green** with envy | |
| the **monster of all monster** pizzas | |
| Sally is **like a kinda Scrooge** | |
| **wolfing** down the pizza | |

# Explaining how words and phrases enhance meaning

Strand:     Language for effect

National Curriculum reference:

- discussing words and phrases that capture the reader's interest and imagination

Reading Test / Content Domain links:   2a, 2b, 2g

# DARK CLOUDS OVERHEAD

Read this poem and think about the words and phrases the writer has chosen.

## The Storm Giant

clouds huddle like an angry mob
as lightning cuts through the air
that's when I hear the grey sky sob
as the light dims in despair
thunder growls at the mountain peaks
like an animal trapped in a cage
the wind in the dull-painted background shrieks
as the storm giant takes to the stage

Answering these questions will help you to think why the particular words were chosen.

1.  How might an **angry mob** behave?

    _____

2.  What comes to mind when we think of something that **cuts**?

    _____

3.  Who or what normally **sobs** and when?

    _____

    _____

4.  When is someone usually **in despair**?

    _____

5.  What **growls**?

    _____

6.  Why is the thunder growling **at the mountain peaks?**

_____

_____

7.  Where might you see a **dull-painted background?**

_____

_____

8.  What sort of person usually **takes to the stage?**

_____

9.  Why do you think the writer called the poem **The Storm Giant?**

_____

_____

Now say what effect the poem had on you.  Try reading it out loud first.

- How did it make you feel?
- Did you like it?
- Was it a good description of a storm?
- How well did the words and phrases create a picture in your mind?

_____

_____

_____

_____

_____

_____

## HOW ABOUT A HOLIDAY?

Many ads in magazines, on television and online hope to persuade you, using words and images, to sign up to a holiday package. Track down the persuasive words and phrases in these two ads and record them in the table below.

> *Do you need a holiday from the weather?*
> *A luxury beachside winter break can be yours at discounted prices in the wonderful Spanish resort of Gran Lanzaria. Our kid-friendly pools are surrounded by oceanview all-day sun terraces.*

> *Luxurious and stylish accommodation awaits you at the 5-star Hotel Extravagance, where*
> *- YOUR LEISURE IS OUR PLEASURE -*
> *With your own superb terrace and raindance shower, what more could you ask for?*

| questions | |
|---|---|
| | |
| adjectives | |
| | |
| made-up words | |
| catchphrases | |

# HOW ABOUT SAVING THE PLANET?

There is a lot written about recycling and how it helps to save the planet and protect wildlife from extinction. Look for evidence of persuasive language in this letter to the council and complete the table below.

> Dear Sir,
>
> Are you one of those uncaring councils that thinks it's ok to let the Polar Bear become extinct? It's innocent and endangered. In my own modest way, I have begun my CARE FOR A BEAR campaign.
>
> Isn't it time the thoughtless members of the council encouraged more recycling? Otherwise, this sad world will be left with one bear clinging helplessly to a single block of ice.
>
> Yours faithfully,
>
> Miss I. Foster

| questions | |
|---|---|
|  |  |
| adjectives |  |
| strong, emotive words |  |
| slogans |  |

© Copyright HeadStart Primary Ltd

108

# Themes and conventions

Strand:     Themes and conventions

**National Curriculum reference:**

- identifying themes and conventions in a wide range of books

**Reading Test / Content Domain links:**   2a, 2b, 2c, 2f, 2g

# MYTHS

The short story below contains lots of the things you find in myths.  It is how you know it is a myth.  Circle the evidence in  the text and link it to the labels on the right.  One has already been done for you.

## Dragonscale

In those days when time itself was hidden in  mist, it was said that the man or  woman who took a shimmering scale from the wing of a dragon would hold the power of flight.

Above the  Forest of Drac, the fiery  breath of the Seven  Dragons of  Brancastle seemed to set the very sky alight.  At the edge of that dark forest, the evil Dragon-master crossed the courtyard of his castle,  frustrated that he hadn't yet been able to acquire a scale for himself.

He needed bait. And when young Garth the blacksmith's son — himself a master of fire — and his sister,  Kate, entered the forest to gather wood, he was overcome by a frenzy of mad laughter.

Pushing Garth  to  the  ground, the  Dragon-master locked Kate in his foul dungeon,  promising to  release  her  only  if  Garth  returned  with  a dragonscale.

Soon, the boy was lost in the maze of forest paths.  That's  when he felt  the  ground  vibrating, heard the  ripping  of  branches from trees and fell to his knees, facing seven pairs of hideous eyes.

He expected death to come quickly,  but no. Recognising one who also knew the ways of fire, one of the dragons stepped forward, and allowed him  to climb up between its wings.  There, he was flown back to the castle, where the Dragon-master shook with fear and set Kate free.

After all, Garth had returned with  a dragon-scale, even though it was still attached to the dragon.

mythical creatures

hero   (good)

villain  (evil)

set in a time

long ago

mysterious setting

good triumphs

over evil

danger has to be

overcome

## THESEUS AND THE MINOTAUR

Search this Greek myth for examples of the themes that are usually present in all myths. Highlight them and link them to the labels on the right. One has already been done for you.

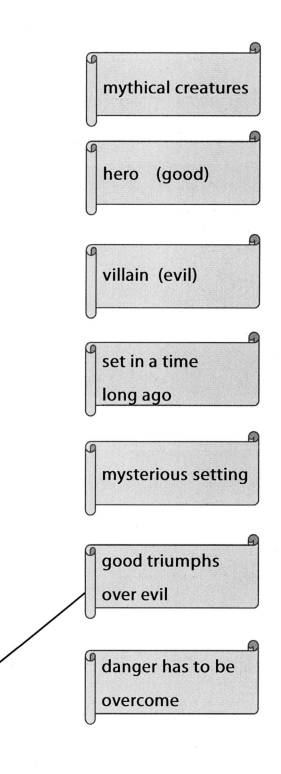

### THESEUS AND THE MINOTAUR

In the days before the gods stopped their meddling in the lives of humans, an old and bitter king, called Minos, ruled the island of Crete. Year after year, he attacked the city of Athens in order to avenge the loss of his son.

At last, he agreed to leave the city in peace if, every nine years, they sent seven girls and seven boys to be sacrificed to the beast called the Minotaur. This was a creature – half man and half bull – that lived in the dark and dismal maze underneath the king's palace.

Then, one year, Prince Theseus stepped forward and offered to go himself. His plan was to track down the Minotaur and kill it, though no one had ever come out of the maze alive.

After arriving on the island, Theseus left the palace to meet Ariadne, the daughter of King Minos. She provided Theseus with a sword and a long piece of string.

Next morning, following Ariadne's plan, Theseus tied one end of the string to the entrance and entered the maze alone. In its deep, bone-littered caverns, he confronted the grotesque monster. There was a fierce battle but, being a skilled and determined fighter, Theseus killed the beast and followed the string back to the outside world and safety.

mythical creatures

hero  (good)

villain  (evil)

set in a time
long ago

mysterious setting

good triumphs
over evil

danger has to be
overcome

## DEAR DIARY

Diaries contain some reference to the date, are written in the 1st person (**I** and **me** not **he** or **she**) and are likely to be in an **informal** style – **not perfect English**. What writers write about can be their **personal feelings, likes and dislikes**, perhaps **dreams** they've remembered from the night before and **hopes** they might have for the future.

## DRAGON'S DIARY

Thursday, 27th April 293 AD

Dear Diary,

Had the most awful dream last night. That pest, with the rusting, clanking suit – George something or other – crept up behind me and shouted BOO! Really gets on my nerves. I'm going to sort him out one of these days. You just can't trust knights nowadays. I haven't forgotten what he said when we first met. If I toasted his bagels for him, then he would put on a show for the villagers of chasing me off. No harm done. Huh! Then Mr Puffycheeks got himself a new lance. Had to show off. Oh, yeah. Couldn't help himself he said. It'll take ages for this tail to get better. I do hope they send someone else soon. Somebody prepared to negotiate, have a chinwag, share a muffin. That'd be nice.

Write down some words and phrases that tells you this is a diary entry:

date of diary entry _____

written in 1st person _____

dreams _____

personal feelings _____

hopes for the future _____

---

# ADVENTURE

In adventure stories, you often find an unlikely person has to be a **hero**, to perform some **dangerous task, rescue** somebody or **solve** some **impossible problem**. There is a lot of **action** written in **short sentences**. There may also be a **cliff-hanger** as well as **hard decisions** to be made by the central characters. Here are two samples of adventure stories. Find some examples of these themes.

> Nasira had never seen herself as the rescuing type. Saving? Wasn't that something the police and fire fighters did? She couldn't save her pocket money. Now here she was – hanging by her fingertips from a drainpipe, peering in the window at the two rough-looking men who had stolen all the money from her grandma's shop. Now, should she phone for help or sneak in once they had left the room? Oh, Nasira, Nasira! Now what?

Now underline evidence of: **unlikely heroine, danger, hard decision, cliff-hanger.**

> Leon checked his watch. He must have checked it only seconds ago. Those hands had barely moved. Where were they? All the guys. The reinforcements. The army, the navy or whoever it was Marek said he was going to fetch. Meanwhile, using binoculars, he could see the stolen World Cup through the window of the power boat. The fog was rolling in. On deck, a member of the crew had already started up the engine. Should he swim out there? Suddenly: heavy footsteps. Someone was coming. Closer and closer. "Hey," said a voice behind him. "Hey, you!"

Now write down evidence of the following themes:

unlikely hero _____

short sentences _____

hard decision _____

danger _____

cliff-hanger _____

# MYSTERY

Mystery stories include **strange events** that need investigating, **secrets, clues, witnesses** who aren't believed at first, **suspects** and **someone to sort it all out**. Can you find any examples of these elements in the following investigation.

## THE HUMMING SHED

Detective Sergeant Morris peered down at Harriet and Jake. They could see he wasn't writing anything in his notebook – more like doodling. What they didn't see was the new neighbour watching from an upstairs window.

"So, this is the shed, is it? The one that you said... what? It hums? Look, kids, I'm trying not to laugh, but really – a shed that hums!"

"Not just humming," insisted Harriet.

"Yesterday," said Jake, "it was at the bottom of the garden. Now it's here, next to the house. Grandad went in on Tuesday, then Dad, Gran and Mum, and they haven't been seen since."

Morris shook his head. "Kids! Too many computer games." He sighed. "Look, let's sort this out once and for all." He reached for the door handle.

"No!" yelled Harriet and Jake together as the weird humming started up and grew louder and louder. A twist of pain travelled across the policeman's face as he slowly disappeared.

Now write down examples of these themes:

**strange event to be investigated** _____

_____

**clues** _____

**witnesses** _____

**suspect** _____

Test Administration Guidance

SCALED SCORE TEST A
Fishface Freddie and Monsters of the Deep / Whale Diary / A Guide to Whales

SCALED SCORE TEST B
Paper Aeroplanes / Icarus / Kites

SCALED SCORE TEST C
Street Party / Flags and Everything / The Dark Horse

Answers, Mark Schemes and Progress Tracking/Scaled Score Information

**PLEASE NOTE:**

**The CD-ROM/digital version also contains the book and tests filed separately for printing. A full answer version and colour digital versions of the book and tests are also included.**

**The raw score/scaled score conversion charts are also supplied.**

Strand:     Range of texts


National Curriculum objectives:


- [listening to and] discussing a wide range of fiction, poetry, plays, non-fiction and reference books or textbooks


- reading books that are structured in different ways and reading for a range of purposes


- increasing their familiarity with a wide range of books, including fairy stories, myths and legends [and retelling some of these orally]

Reading Test / Content Domain links:   2a, 2b, 2c, 2d, 2e, 2f, 2g

A note about the tests:

The KS2 English Reading Test Framework 2016 (table 9) sets out the proportion of marks for each domain, with the higher percentages given to **retrieving and recording information** and **making inferences**. This is reflected in the test questions presented here.

## Year 4 Reading Comprehension - Test Admin Guidance

## Before Starting the Test

Explain to the children that the questions require different kinds of answers.

- The space for the answer shows the type of answer required. Some questions require a one word/short answer and others require a longer answer.

- For some questions, a different type of answer is required e.g. circling/ticking an answer or joining two items together with a line.

- The number underneath the line on the right-hand side of each question indicates how many marks there are for each question.

## Timing

The Year 4 tests are not intended to be strictly timed tests, so please allow as much time as necessary. If appropriate, the tests can be stopped and re-started as long as pupils do not have a chance to share/discuss the test content. It may be appropriate to split a test over two or more sessions.

## Equipment

Each pupil will need a pencil or pen.

A rubber can be used but crossing out is preferable as long as answers remain legible.

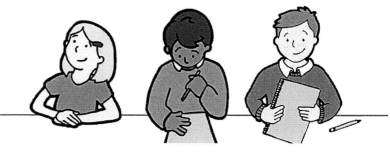

© Copyright HeadStart Primary Ltd.

## Assistance

General instructions on the test papers may be read to children. Instructions may also be re-phrased as long as no inappropriate assistance is given.

In Year 4, it may be appropriate for some children to read the texts and questions aloud if this is part of normal classroom practice. This should happen in a different room than children completing the tests silently.

## Children with Special Needs or Disabilities

If children need specific kinds of assistance, equipment or environment to complete the tests, this should be provided as long as it is part of normal classroom practice.

© Copyright HeadStart Primary Ltd.

# HeadStart
## Primary

## Reading Comprehension

YEAR 4

## Scaled Score TEST A

Name: .......................................................................................

Class: ........................................................................................

Date: .........................................................................................

Raw Score .................. /50

Scaled Score ...................

# FISHFACE FREDDIE AND MONSTERS OF THE DEEP

You know, Captain Nell, I've been at sea, man and boy, for sixty years. And I've seen some unusual happenings.

Wow, that's a long time, Fishface! I imagine you've come across blue whales and great white sharks.

Much more. I've seen sea serpents, enormous jellyfish the size of islands and monsters as big as a rugby pitch.

Are you sure you didn't dream it all? You know the biggest jellyfish is eight feet wide and there are giant squids.

Sailing from Norway to Greenland, I was, when I glanced out at sea and saw an ugly thing staring back at me.

Was the sea calm and like a mirror? Did I tell you about the time I came face to face with a Freddiesquid?

1

© Copyright HeadStart Primary Ltd.

1. How long has Fishface Freddie been at sea?

..............................................................................

1 mark

2. Circle the word that means the same as **strange**.

unusual          ugly          imagine

1 mark

3. Fishface Freddie has been at sea longer than Captain Nell. What does Captain Nell say that tells you this?

..............................................................................

1 mark

4. Write down the **three** creatures that Fishface Freddie says he has seen.

1. ..........................................................

2. ..........................................................

3. ..........................................................

2 marks

5. Write down a word that means the same as **enormous.**

..........................................................

1 mark

**2**

**6** Write down the **two** phrases that Fishface Freddie uses to describe how big he says the creatures were.

**1.**
...................................................................................

**2.**
...................................................................................

2 marks

**7** Captain Nell doesn't believe what he says about monsters. How do you know?

...................................................................................

...................................................................................

1 mark

**8** Captain Nell suggests **two** real creatures Fishface Freddie might have seen. What are they?

**1.**
.........................................................................

**2.**
.........................................................................

1 mark

**9** Captain Nell says that jellyfish can be big. How big?

...................................................................................

1 mark

**10** Where does Fishface Freddie say he was when he saw these monsters?

...................................................................................

1 mark

**3**

© Copyright HeadStart Primary Ltd.

**11** Freddie says that he **glanced out at sea**. What does **glanced** mean? **Tick one**.

sailed ☐

rowed ☐

looked ☐

1 mark

**12** What do you think the **ugly thing** was that Freddie saw?

........................................................................

1 mark

**13** When Captain Nell asks if the sea was calm, what does she compare the sea to?

........................................................

1 mark

**14** What is Captain Nell doing when she talks about the time she came **face to face with a Freddiesquid?** **Tick one**.

telling Freddie a true story ☐

playing a joke on Freddie ☐

1 mark

**4**

Page Total

© Copyright HeadStart Primary Ltd.

# WHALE DIARY

The owner of this diary had a holiday on a boat whale-watching.

> **Monday 1st June 2015**
> Conditions: sunny, breezy, small breaking waves.
> Once on board, I felt like a 5 year old on my first adventure. Since seeing the captain's photos of these mighty beasts, we were all fizzing with
>
> excitement. 11am A pod of white-beaked dolphins amused us all with their acrobatics alongside the boat. By then, I'd stopped imagining every crest of a wave was a minke whale. But, luckily, returning to harbour, I saw

**1** What was the weather like on 1st June 2015?

.................................................................................

*1 mark*

**2** How do you know the writer is excited as he steps on board the boat? What does he say?

.................................................................................

.................................................................................

*1 mark*

**3** What are the **mighty beasts**?

.................................................................................

*1 mark*

**5**

**Page Total**

© Copyright HeadStart Primary Ltd.

④ The writer also tries to describe his excitement using a sound. What is it?

..............................................

1 mark

⑤ The writer wasn't whale-watching alone.
How do you know?

..............................................

1 mark

⑥ At what time of day were the dolphins spotted?

..............................................

1 mark

⑦ **Circle one word** that means the same as **pod**.

game          group          baby

1 mark

⑧ What word does the writer use to describe dolphins jumping out of the sea?

..............................................

1 mark

⑨ What does the writer mistake for a minke whale?

..............................................

1 mark

6

Page Total

© Copyright HeadStart Primary Ltd.

**10** What do you think is on the next page of the diary?

The writer might say something about:

- what he saw

- how he felt

- what was special about the holiday

**What he saw:**

...............................................................................................

...............................................................................................

...............................................................................................

**How he felt:**

...............................................................................................

...............................................................................................

...............................................................................................

**What was special about the holiday:**

...............................................................................................

...............................................................................................

...............................................................................................

...............................................................................................

3 marks

**11** If you hadn't read the title at the top of the page, how would you know this was from a diary?

Write down **two** things.

**1.** ...............................................................................................

**2.** ...............................................................................................

2 marks

Page Total

# A GUIDE TO WHALES

| whale | size | food | offspring | special notes |
|---|---|---|---|---|
| **Blue Whale** | Grows to 105 feet or 32 metres. Weight = 190 tons or the same as 20 or more African elephants. Females are larger than males. | Instead of teeth, they have rows of comb-like plates for filtering krill and small fish out of the water. Can eat 4 tons of food each day. | 23 feet at birth or 7 metres and 3 tons, babies drink up to 150 gallons of mother's milk every day. | Largest and loudest mammal. They make a low whistle heard for 100s of miles. Can live up to 80 years. |
| **Minke Whale** | Up to 35 feet or 10.7 metres. Weight = 7-11 tons. Females are slightly larger. | Without teeth and a solitary hunter, its food includes krill and small fish. | 9 feet or almost 3 metres and ½ ton. | Can live up to 50 years. Very curious and swim close to boats. |
| **Orca** | Males grow up to 30 feet or just over 9 metres; females are 25 feet or 7.6 metres. Weight = 7-10 tons. | A toothed whale, it eats fish, squid, birds and sea mammals. They work in groups and track prey by echo-location (bouncing sound off objects). | 7 feet or around 2 metres and 400 pounds. Babies stay with mother for 2 years. Pods (groups) are led by females. | Also known as killer whales, they are the largest of the dolphin family of sea mammals. Live 30 – 50 years. Groups can number as many as 100 orcas. |

© Copyright HeadStart Primary Ltd.

**1** The blue whale is very big. What does the writer compare it to?

......................................................................................... 1 mark

**2** What size is a blue whale when it is born?

......................................................................................... 1 mark

**3** The blue whale makes a low whistle sound.
How far away can it be heard?

......................................................................................... 1 mark

**4** How much food can a blue whale eat in one day?

......................................................................................... 1 mark

**5** If you wanted to add the fact that the blue whale's heart is as big as a small car, which heading might you put it under?
**Circle one**.

whale          size          food

offspring          special notes          1 mark

**6** What is the other name for the orca?

......................................................................................... 1 mark

Page Total

© Copyright HeadStart Primary Ltd.

**7** Which whale has teeth? **Circle one**.

blue whale          orca          minke whale

*1 mark*

**8** As well as giving birth to babies and looking after them, in what other way is the female orca very important?

..................................................................
*1 mark*

**9** How do orcas find their food?  Find and write down **two** things they do.

**1.** .............................................................

**2.** .............................................................
*2 marks*

**10** Why has the writer put **(bouncing sound off objects)** in brackets?

..................................................................
*1 mark*

**11** How long can a minke whale live?

..................................................................
*1 mark*

Page Total

© Copyright HeadStart Primary Ltd.

**12** What is it about minke whales that makes them easier to spot when whale-watching?

.............................................................

.............................................................

1 mark

**13** What does the minke whale eat?  Write down **two things**.

**1.** ...........................................

**2.** ...........................................

2 marks

**14** Write down another word or phrase that means the same as **offspring**.

.............................................................

1 mark

**15** **Tick** whether the following statements are **true** or **false**.

| statement | true | false |
|---|---|---|
| The blue whale is the biggest because it eats small sea mammals. | | |
| Minke whales hunt in groups. | | |
| Orcas can live for 45 years. | | |

2 marks

**Page Total**

© Copyright HeadStart Primary Ltd.

**16** **Draw a line** to match each whale with the description of its size.

larger than male orca

female orca

same size as male orca

smaller than male orca

larger than female minke

male minke

same size as female minke

smaller than female minke

2 marks

_____

**End of TEST A**

**Page Total**

© Copyright HeadStart Primary Ltd.

# Reading Comprehension

## YEAR 4

## Scaled Score TEST B

Name:
........................................................................

Class:
........................................................................

Date:
........................................................................

**Raw Score** ................. / 50

**Scaled Score** .................

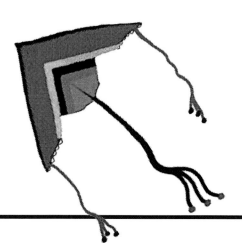

# PAPER AEROPLANES

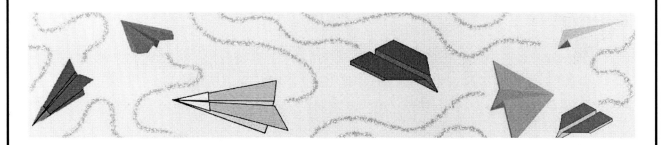

## IT'S A RECORD

The longest time a paper aeroplane has stayed in the air (inside, over level ground) was set in December 2010 by Takuo Toda of Japan. His aeroplane stayed up for 29.2 seconds. The farthest distance a paper aeroplane has been thrown (inside over level ground) is 69.14 metres. This was achieved by Joe Ayoob in the USA in 2012.

[**Please note**: records were correct at the time this was written.]

## HOW TO MAKE A SIMPLE PAPER AEROPLANE

**Equipment needed**

1 piece of A4 paper – colour of your choice.
A ruler to help with folds.

**Step-by-step Guide**

First: fold along the length of the paper. **(1)** Open it out again – this fold is called a guide fold to help in later stages.

Second: fold down the 2 corners as shown in the diagram. **(2)**

Third: fold in the new *shoulders*. **(3)**

Fourth: fold shape **(4)** in half. See **(5)**. You should now have reached diagram **(6)**.

Fifth: fold back the new *shoulders*. **(7)** Your aeroplane **(8)** is ready for take-off! **(9)**

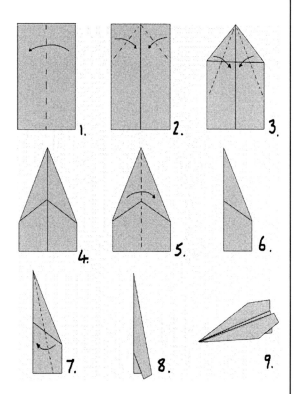

1
© Copyright HeadStart Primary Ltd.

**1** Why is **IT'S A RECORD** a good title for the first text?

..................................................................

..................................................................

1 mark

**2** Takuo Toda set a record.  How long did his paper aeroplane stay in the air?

..................................................................

1 mark

**3** Anyone trying to break the record has to stick to the rules. The writer says what the rules are.  **Tick one**.

**stayed in the air**

**inside, over level ground**

**farthest distance**

1 mark

**4** In which country did Joe Ayoob break the record?

..................................................................

1 mark

**5** What is the farthest distance a paper aeroplane has been thrown?

..................................................................

1 mark

**Page Total**

© Copyright HeadStart Primary Ltd.

**6** In **IT'S A RECORD**, why is there a note at the end saying, **records were correct at the time this was written**?

.........................................................................

.........................................................................

1 mark

**7** What kind of text is **HOW TO MAKE A SIMPLE PAPER AEROPLANE**? **Tick one**.

**Instructions** ☐

**Diary** ☐

**Letter** ☐

1 mark

**8** In **HOW TO MAKE A SIMPLE PAPER AEROPLANE**, there are words that tell you what kind of text it is. **Tick three**.

**HOW TO MAKE . . .** ☐

**AEROPLANE** ☐

**Equipment needed** ☐

**colour** ☐

**Step-by-step Guide** ☐

3 marks

**Page Total** ◯

© Copyright HeadStart Primary Ltd.

**9** What piece of equipment will help you to make the folds?

...............................................

1 mark

**10** Why has the writer written the word *shoulders* in italics?

.......................................................................

1 mark

**11** In the **Step-by-step Guide**, what is the last thing you have to do before your aeroplane is ready to fly?

**Tick one**.

**Fold down the corners**

**Fold back the new shoulders**

**Fold it in half**

1 mark

**12** What is it about making paper aeroplanes that makes them popular?

**1.**
...............................................................

**2.**
...............................................................

2 marks

**Page Total**

© Copyright HeadStart Primary Ltd.

# ICARUS

## BACKGROUND INFORMATION...

Icarus's father was called Daedalus. He was known in ancient Greece as a brilliant inventor and sculptor.

He worked on the island of Crete for King Minos. He invented masts and sails for ships. This helped Crete have a strong navy. Also, his sculptures were so lifelike, it was said that they had to be chained to the walls of the palace to stop them escaping.

## THE STORY SO FAR...

Underneath King Minos's palace, in a dark maze, lived a monster called the Minotaur. Daedalus provided the thread that Theseus used to tie to the door of the maze (or labyrinth) so that he could find his way out after slaying the Minotaur. Minos was furious that his pet monster had been killed and he threw Daedalus and his son, Icarus, into the labyrinth.

**1** What was the name of Icarus's father?

................................................................

1 mark

**2** Find and write down the **two** things, invented by Icarus's father, that helped King Minos's navy.

**1.**
................................................................

**2.**
................................................................

1 mark

**5**          **Page Total**

© Copyright HeadStart Primary Ltd.

**3** How does the writer emphasise how lifelike
the sculptures were?

..............................................................................

..............................................................................

2 marks

**4** Look at **The Story So Far**. Where did the Minotaur live?

..............................................................................

1 mark

**5** How did Daedalus help Theseus?

..............................................................................

..............................................................................

2 marks

**6** Find and write down another word for **maze**.

..............................................................

1 mark

Page Total

© Copyright HeadStart Primary Ltd.

# ICARUS (PART 2)

## WHAT HAPPENED NEXT ...

It wasn't so difficult for Daedalus to find his way through the labyrinth. After all, he was the one who had built it. Daedalus knew that he and Icarus had to leave the island and get away from King Minos. But King Minos now controlled the sea around Crete, so escape by boat was impossible. Also, his soldiers patrolled all the roads. Daedalus realised that the only way out was by air. But there was a problem. Flying was only for the gods!

## AND THEN FINALLY ...

So Daedalus made wings for himself and Icarus, using feathers held together with wax. Daedalus warned Icarus not to fly too close to the sun, as it would melt his wings, and not too close to the sea, as it would dampen them and make it hard to fly. Forgetting his father's advice, Icarus flew too close to the sun god, Helios. The wax holding his wings together melted. He flapped his arms, but it was no use. He fell and drowned in the sea.

**7** Why was it easy for Daedalus to find his way through the labyrinth?

..........................................................................................

*1 mark*

**8** **'Daedalus realised that the only way out was by air.'**
Find and write down **two** reasons why this was.

**1.**
..........................................................................................
**2.**
..........................................................................................

*2 marks*

**7**

**Page Total**

© Copyright HeadStart Primary Ltd.

**9** **What Happened Next** ends with: **'Flying was only for the gods!'**

What do you think the writer means by this?

. . . . . . . . . . . . . . . . . . . . . . . . . . . . . . . . . . . . . . . . . . . . . . . . . . .

1 mark

**10** What was the name of the sun god?

. . . . . . . . . . . . . . . . . . . . . . . . . . . . . . . . . .

1 mark

**11** What were the **two** dangers of flying too close to the sun and the sea?

**Sun:**
. . . . . . . . . . . . . . . . . . . . . . . . . . . . . . . . . . . . . . . . . . . . . . . . . . .

. . . . . . . . . . . . . . . . . . . . . . . . . . . . . . . . . . . . . . . . . . . . . . . . . . .

**Sea:**
. . . . . . . . . . . . . . . . . . . . . . . . . . . . . . . . . . . . . . . . . . . . . . . . . . .

. . . . . . . . . . . . . . . . . . . . . . . . . . . . . . . . . . . . . . . . . . . . . . . . . . .

2 marks

**12** **Circle two things** that are an important part of Greek myths.

strange creatures

wings

sculptures

gods

2 marks

Page Total

© Copyright HeadStart Primary Ltd.

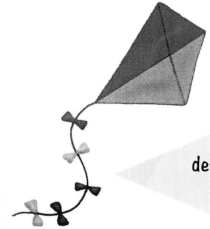

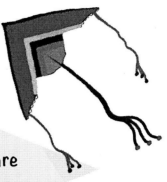

# KITES

Kites are designed to defy gravity and fly but they are always controlled by cords at ground level.

## HISTORY

Kites were invented in the 5th century BC in China, where silk and paper were first made. Silk was both light and strong. This made it ideal for the sail as well as the line held by the handler. Lightweight bamboo was also used for the frame of the kite. Chinese kites were flat and rectangular, but decorated with mythical figures. Some had whistles attached to make musical sounds.

## KITES TODAY

Nowadays, kites are flown for fun in the park, at the beach – anywhere with wide open spaces. They can be flown as part of an art show, for sport or simply to demonstrate the skill of the handler.

## SOME USES IN HISTORY

Kites have been used to carry messages, measure distances and test the strength of the wind. In medieval times, the Chinese army used silk kites to lift men up in the air, so that signals could be sent during battle.

## FIREHAWK KITE

Go one better with one of our amazing superhero kites. Any one of our crazy, crafted creations will dominate the sky. Firehawk, in cloud-hugging flight, is quite hypnotic. An artist's dream of colour, movement and jaw-dropping beauty.

9

© Copyright HeadStart Primary Ltd.

**1** In the **HISTORY** section, what other word could have been used instead of **ideal**? **Circle one.**

cheap          perfect          strong

1 mark

**2** In China, they had **three** materials that were very useful for making kites. What were they?

**1.** ........................................................

**2.** ........................................................

**3.** ........................................................

3 marks

**3** What shape were ancient Chinese kites?

........................................................

1 mark

**4** In ancient China, how might people have known a kite was in the air, even if they weren't able to see it?

........................................................

1 mark

**5** Look at what the **HISTORY** section is about. Think of another title that would help a reader know what it is about.

........................................................

1 mark

**10**

Page Total

© Copyright HeadStart Primary Ltd.

**6** Find and write down **three** ways in which kites have been used in history.

**1.** ...................................................................................

**2.** ...................................................................................

**3.** ...................................................................................

3 marks

**7** In **KITES TODAY**, the phrase **'demonstrating the skill of the handler'** is used.

What other phrase might have been used? **Tick one.**

**teaching someone to fly a kite** ☐

**getting better at flying a kite** ☐

**showing how well you fly a kite** ☐

1 mark

**8** Why are the park and the beach good places to fly a kite?

..........................................................................................

1 mark

**9** Write **fact** or **opinion** after these sentences.

**Kites were invented in China.** ...............................

**Kites are flown in the park.** ...............................

**Firehawk is quite hypnotic.** ...............................

2 marks

11

Page Total

**10** What is meant by **cloud-hugging** in the **Firehawk Kite** advert?

................................................................................................

1 mark

**11** Pick out 3 words in the **Firehawk Kite** advert that are there to try to persuade you to buy a kite.

**1.**
................................................................

**2.**
................................................................

**3.**
................................................................

3 marks

---

**End of TEST B**

Page Total

© Copyright HeadStart Primary Ltd.

# Reading Comprehension

## YEAR 4

## Scaled Score TEST C

Name: ........................................................................................

Class: ....................................................................................

Date: .....................................................................................

Raw Score ................ /50

Scaled Score ....................

## STREET PARTY

### Street Party

**27 June 12 noon - 7:30pm**

FUN for the whole family!

**BANDS - CHOIRS - SCHOOL ORCHESTRA**

Our street is now free of cars. Let's celebrate!

**Kids' Activities - Splat the Rat - Face-painting - Lucky Dip - Ugliest Pet Competition - Penalty Shoot-out**

Raffle winners announced by the Mayor's wife at 5:30pm. Prizes generously donated by Frank's Newsagent, The Frothy Coffee Shop, Abigail's Antiques and Happy Valley Garden Centre.

Admission is free, but you can give £2 as a donation to our Red Nose Day appeal and get a free raffle ticket + programme.

In the event of rain, the party will be held in the school hall.

---

**1** On this poster, why are the words **Street Party** bigger than the others?

.............................................................................

1 mark

**2** What age of people is the writer hoping to persuade to come to the street party?

.............................................................................

1 mark

**3** How much does it cost to get in?

.............................................................................

1 mark

**1**

**Page Total**

© Copyright HeadStart Primary Ltd.

**4** Why is the street party happening?

................................................................

................................................................

1 mark

**5** If you donate £2, what will you get in return?

................................................................

1 mark

**6** How is the Frothy Coffee Shop helping the party attract lots of people?

................................................................

1 mark

**7** **'Prizes generously donated . . .'**

**Circle** a word that means the same as **donated**.

given          bought          won

1 mark

**8** When will you find out if you've won the raffle?

................................................................

1 mark

**9** Who will announce the winner of the raffle?

................................................................

1 mark

**2**

Page Total

© Copyright HeadStart Primary Ltd.

**10** Why is **Splat the Rat** an easy phrase to remember?

...................................................................................

1 mark

**11** What is going to happen if the weather is bad?

...................................................................................

1 mark

**Page Total**

© Copyright HeadStart Primary Ltd.

# FLAGS AND EVERYTHING

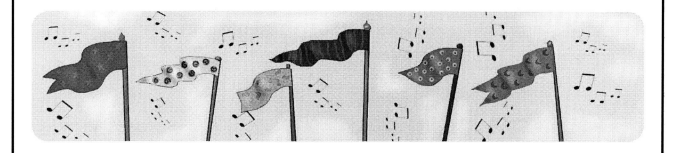

Here is part of a letter:

The flags and everything made it look just like a proper funfair, Gran.  Dad said you were good at the coconut shy when you took him.  Did you go to funfairs when you were little?  Maybe they didn't have them during the war.  Did your school have anything like that?  Our teacher was in charge of Splat the Rat.  You have a drainpipe and somebody drops a rat (not a real one) in the top and when it comes out the bottom you have to try and hit it with a hammer.  I kept missing but it was still fun.  I did win some chocolates in the lucky dip.  I'll bring them next time I come, if I have any left.

Lots of love,
Rita x

P.S. Hope you feel better soon.

© Copyright HeadStart Primary Ltd.

**1** Who is Rita writing to?

.................................................................... 1 mark

**2** What is Rita writing about?

.................................................................... 1 mark

**3** What did the flags remind Rita of?

.................................................................... 1 mark

**4** Who used to be good at the coconut shy?
**Circle one**.

Rita          Dad          Gran

1 mark

**5** Who was in charge of Splat the Rat?

.................................................................... 1 mark

**6** Why do you think she put **(not a real one)** in brackets?

.................................................................... 1 mark

**7** How do you know that Rita enjoyed Splat the Rat?

.................................................................... 1 mark

Page Total

© Copyright HeadStart Primary Ltd.

**8** What did Rita win?

..................................................................

1 mark

**9** Why do you think the person she is writing to didn't

go with her?

..................................................................

1 mark

**10** If you hadn't been told this was part of a letter, which **two**

clues would tell you that it was?

**1.** ..............................................................

**2.** ..............................................................

2 marks

**Page Total**

© Copyright HeadStart Primary Ltd.

# THE DARK HORSE

Greta, she's my sister, gave me one of her looks. You know, one of those 'I'm two years older than you, so I know best' looks.

"Jacob, this is my thirteenth birthday today. We've come to the fair to enjoy ourselves. This carousel is amazing. So stop being so grumpy and cheer up."

I sighed and did a crazy, cross-eyed smile. "Is that better?" I said. Greta didn't answer, but stomped off towards the candy floss stall.

The trouble was: England was okay. My new school was okay. I liked our new house near the seaside. Mum and Dad kept telling me how lucky I was. But it wasn't home. It wasn't the country I had grown up in. I was homesick.

Now that Greta had wandered off, I peered up at the wooden carousel horses, brightly painted and glinting in the sun. One in particular, a shiny, sleek horse, was as black as the night, with rainbow decorations. It looked as if it wanted to break free of its bolts and, by some magic, take to the air.

The name painted on its neck was Moonrider.

7

© Copyright HeadStart Primary Ltd.

**1** Who is telling the story?

..............................................................................

1 mark

**2** How do you know who is telling the story?

..............................................................................

..............................................................................

1 mark

**3** How old is Greta?

.......................................................

1 mark

**4** What is the word that is used to show how annoyed Greta was when she left?

..............................................................................

1 mark

**5** Where did Greta go when she left?

.......................................................

1 mark

**6** Although Jacob liked his new house near the seaside, how did he feel?

..............................................................................

1 mark

**Page Total**

© Copyright HeadStart Primary Ltd.

**7** **Circle** a word that means the same as **glinting**.

sparkling          sprinting          gliding

1 mark

**8** Jacob is interested in one of the wooden carousel horses. What is its name?

...............................................

1 mark

**9** Jacob describes the wooden horses as being brightly painted. Write down **two** things he says about the colour of one horse in particular.

**1.**
....................................................................................

**2.**
....................................................................................

2 marks

**10** Jacob says there was something magical about the horse, as if it wanted to **take to the air**.

What is meant by **take to the air**?

....................................................................................

1 mark

**Page Total**

© Copyright HeadStart Primary Ltd.

# THE DARK HORSE - PART 2

I climbed up, stood beside it and ran my hand along its saddle.

"You don't want that one, lad." The carousel owner snarled like a cornered fox. He shook his head and pushed back his oily, red hair. "Nobody ever goes on that one. It doesn't earn me any money. I'm getting rid of it tonight."

The painted eye of Moonrider stared at me and, as soon as the owner left, I couldn't help myself climbing on.

The whirling music started up. I felt the rise and fall of the galloper. People and sideshows and the fields around whizzed by, until I stopped seeing them. Another rising up of my wooden steed beneath me and I suddenly felt free of the carousel, the fairground and this new country I had come to.

We were flying over hills I used to climb and the river I used to swim in, with distant, snow-capped mountains beyond. There was our old farm far below. All the familiar places. Then Moonrider turned and I found myself on the carousel again as it slowly came to a standstill.

Leaving the fair, I put my hand on Greta's arm. "Wait," I said, smiling. "One last look." As I looked back at the dark, mysterious horse, I thought, maybe I'll come back again tomorrow.

**10**

© Copyright HeadStart Primary Ltd.

**11** There are **two** things the carousel owner says to Jacob to try to put him off choosing Moonrider. What are they?

1. ...............................................................................................

2. ...............................................................................................

2 marks

**12** Why has the owner decided to get rid of the carousel horse?

......................................................................................................

......................................................................................................

1 mark

**13** The carousel owner **snarled**. What animal is he compared to?

......................................................................................................

1 mark

**14** What word does the writer use to suggest the sound of carousel music?

......................................................................................................

1 mark

**15** Look at the paragraph that begins:

**The whirling music started up. I felt the ...**

Find and write down **two** words that are used instead of 'horse'.

1. ..............................................................

2. ..............................................................

2 marks

**11**

**Page Total**

**16** Once the carousel started up, **three** things whizzed by.
What were they?

**1.**
.............................................................

**2.**
.............................................................

**3.**
.............................................................

2 marks

**17** Jacob said, **'I suddenly felt free . . .'**
There are **three** things he felt free from.  What are they?

**1.**
.............................................................

**2.**
.............................................................

**3.**
.............................................................

2 marks

**18** The main idea in the 2nd last paragraph has to do with Jacob
seeing places he once knew.  Find **three** phrases that add
more detail.

**1.**
.............................................................

**2.**
.............................................................

**3.**
.............................................................

3 marks

**19** What is the meaning of: **came to a standstill**?  **Circle one**.

| stopped | turned | climbed |

1 mark

**12**

Page Total

© Copyright HeadStart Primary Ltd.

**20** Jacob feels a lot happier at the end.  How do you know?

.........................................................................................

.........................................................................................

1 mark

**21** If the owner of the carousel was going to get rid of
Moonrider, what do you think Jacob would do about it?

.........................................................................................

.........................................................................................

1 mark

---

**End of TEST C**

**Page Total**

© Copyright HeadStart Primary Ltd.

# YEAR 4

# Reading Comprehension

## ANSWERS & MARK SCHEME

### Scaled Score TESTS A, B & C

# Tracking - using tests to track children's progress

Once a test has been marked, a raw score out of 50 can be awarded.
This score should then be converted to a scaled score using the conversion charts in the digital/CD-ROM version.

The table below can then be used to identify progress against one of the 6 stages.
(See notes in the digital/CD-ROM version for further information.)

**Year 4**

NB: The stage boundaries and 3 'standards' in the table below are intended as a guide to children's progress. They should not be interpreted in the same way as a scaled score of 100 is used as 'standard met' in KS1 and KS2 SATs.

| Scaled Score | Stage | |
|---|---|---|
| 0 - 75 | Emerging | Working towards the expected standard |
| 76 - 95 | Developing | |
| | | |
| 96 - 100 | Progressing | Working within the expected standard |
| 101 - 112 | Secure | |
| | | |
| 113 - 122 | Exceeding | Working above the expected standard |
| 123 + | Exceeding with greater depth | |

The assessments are intended to be used by teachers as a tool to support their professional judgement. The table above should be used only as a guide to achievement and progress. This data should always be used in conjunction with ongoing teacher assessment.

1

© Copyright HeadStart Primary Ltd.

The text and table below are taken directly from the 'Key Stage 2 English reading test framework'. This document is used by test designers to create the Key Stage 2 SAT.

The appropriate 'domains' are identified in the following HeadStart mark scheme.

# 4. Content domain

The content domain sets out the relevant elements from the national curriculum programme of study (2014) for English at key stage 2 that are assessed in the English reading test. The tests will, over time, sample from each area of the content domain.

The key stage 2 English reading tests will focus on the comprehension elements of the national curriculum.

Table 2 shows the content domain, which sets out how elements of the curriculum will be defined for test development purposes.

**Table 2: Content domain relating to questions**

| | Content domain reference |
|---|---|
| **2a** | give / explain the meaning of words in context |
| **2b** | retrieve and record information / identify key details from fiction and non-fiction |
| **2c** | summarise main ideas from more than one paragraph |
| **2d** | make inferences from the text / explain and justify inferences with evidence from the text |
| **2e** | predict what might happen from details stated and implied |
| **2f** | identify / explain how information / narrative content is related and contributes to meaning as a whole |
| **2g** | identify / explain how meaning is enhanced through choice of words and phrases |
| **2h** | make comparisons within the text |

2

© Copyright HeadStart Primary Ltd.

## Fishface Freddie and Monsters of the Deep

| No. | Answers and Mark Scheme | Domain | Marks |
|---|---|---|---|
| 1 | sixty years | 2b | 1 |
| 2 | unusual | 2a | 1 |
| 3 | 'Wow, that's a long time, Fishface!' | 2d | 1 |
| 4 | sea serpents, (enormous) jellyfish, monsters **[Award 2 marks for three correct answers; 1 mark for two correct answers.]** | 2b | 2 |
| 5 | big / huge / gigantic, etc. | 2a | 1 |
| 6 | the size of islands = 1 mark as big as a rugby pitch = 1 mark | 2g | 2 |
| 7 | 'Are you sure you didn't dream it all?' (She says.) | 2d | 1 |
| 8 | blue whale, great white shark, jellyfish, giant squid **[Award 1 mark for any two correct answers.]** | 2d | 1 |
| 9 | eight feet wide | 2b | 1 |
| 10 | Sailing from Norway to Greenland | 2b | 1 |
| 11 | looked | 2a | 1 |
| 12 | his own reflection / face | 2d | 1 |
| 13 | a mirror | 2g | 1 |
| 14 | playing a joke on Freddie | 2d | 1 |

© Copyright HeadStart Primary Ltd.

## Whale Diary

| No. | Answers and Mark Scheme | Domain | Marks |
|---|---|---|---|
| 1 | sunny, breezy, (small breaking waves) | 2b | 1 |
| 2 | 'I felt like a 5 year old (on my first adventure).' | 2g | 1 |
| 3 | whales | 2g | 1 |
| 4 | fizzing | 2g | 1 |
| 5 | use of **we** and / or **us** | 2d | 1 |
| 6 | 11am | 2b | 1 |
| 7 | group | 2a | 1 |
| 8 | acrobatics | 2g | 1 |
| 9 | every crest of a wave | 2d | 1 |
| 10 | more minke whales / even bigger, unexpected whale - excited, etc. - memorable / once in a lifetime holiday, etc. more dolphins / no whales - disappointed - hoping next trip will be better / but happy enough<br>**[Award 1 mark for every attempt to answer the bulleted points in the question.]** | 2e | 3 |
| 11 | date (time) / use of first person (I) / personal thoughts and feelings<br>**[Award 1 mark for each correct answer up to a total of 2 marks.]** | 2f | 2 |

4

© Copyright HeadStart Primary Ltd.

## A Guide to Whales

| No. | Answers and Mark Scheme | Domain | Marks |
|---|---|---|---|
| 1 | (20 or more) African elephants | 2b | 1 |
| 2 | 23 feet / 7 metres | 2b | 1 |
| 3 | 100s of miles | 2b | 1 |
| 4 | 4 tons | 2b | 1 |
| 5 | size<br>**[Accept: special notes]** | 2f | 1 |
| 6 | killer whale | 2b | 1 |
| 7 | orca | 2b | 1 |
| 8 | females lead the pod / are leaders / in charge | 2b | 1 |
| 9 | work in groups = 1 mark<br>use echo-location = 1 mark | 2b | 2 |
| 10 | To explain what **echo-location** means. | 2g | 1 |
| 11 | (up to) 50 years | 2b | 1 |
| 12 | curious / swim close to boats | 2b | 1 |
| 13 | krill = 1 mark<br>small fish = 1 mark | 2b | 2 |
| 14 | babies / children / young | 2a | 1 |
| 15 | The blue whale is the biggest because it eats small sea mammals. ------------------------------- **false**   [1 mark for 2 correct.]<br>Minke whales hunt in groups. ------------------- **false**<br>Orcas can live for 45 years. ------------------------- **true** | 2b | 2 |
| 16 | female orca -------------- smaller than male orca = 1 mark<br>male minke -------------- smaller than female minke = 1 mark | 2b | 2 |

| | TOTAL | 50 |
|---|---|---|

5

© Copyright HeadStart Primary Ltd.

## Paper Aeroplanes

| No. | Answers and Mark Scheme | Domain | Marks |
|---|---|---|---|
| 1 | The text is all about attempts to break (time / distance) records. | 2c | 1 |
| 2 | 29.2 seconds | 2b | 1 |
| 3 | inside, over level ground | 2b | 1 |
| 4 | USA | 2b | 1 |
| 5 | 69.14 metres | 2b | 1 |
| 6 | Perhaps a new record has been set / is being set at this very moment. | 2d | 1 |
| 7 | Instructions | 2f | 1 |
| 8 | HOW TO MAKE . . . = 1 mark<br>Equipment needed = 1 mark<br>Step-by-step guide = 1 mark | 2f | 3 |
| 9 | ruler | 2b | 1 |
| 10 | To distinguish features from corners / an attempt to be clear / they  resemble human shoulders | 2g | 1 |
| 11 | Fold back the new shoulders | 2c | 1 |
| 12 | They are easy / quick to make / not much equipment is needed / you can use scrap paper / if it doesn't work, you can easily make another one / it's fun comparing how well different designs fly<br>**[Award 2 marks for any two correct answers; 1 mark for one correct answer.]** | 2d | 2 |

6

© Copyright HeadStart Primary Ltd.

## Icarus

| No. | Answers and Mark Scheme | Domain | Marks |
|---|---|---|---|
| 1 | Daedalus | 2b | 1 |
| 2 | masts and sails<br>**[Both answers required for 1 mark.]** | 2b | 1 |
| 3 | they had to be chained (to the walls of the palace) **[= 1 mark]** to stop them escaping **[=1 mark]** | 2g | 2 |
| 4 | Underneath King Minos's palace / in the maze / labyrinth | 2b | 1 |
| 5 | He provided Theseus with the thread **[= 1 mark]** which he used to find his way out of the maze. **[= 1 mark]** | 2b | 2 |
| 6 | labyrinth | 2a | 1 |

## Icarus (part 2)

| No. | Answers and Mark Scheme | Domain | Marks |
|---|---|---|---|
| 7 | He (Daedalus) had built it. | 2b | 1 |
| 8 | King Minos controlled the sea (around Crete, so that escape by boat was impossible.) = **1 mark**<br>His soldiers patrolled all the roads. = **1 mark** | 2b | 2 |
| 9 | It's a warning / foreseeing what lies ahead / Daedalus and Icarus weren't gods | 2d | 1 |
| 10 | Helios | 2b | 1 |
| 11 | Sun: it would melt wax / wings = **1 mark**<br>Sea: it would dampen the wings and make it hard to fly = **1 mark** | 2b | 2 |
| 12 | strange creatures = **1 mark**<br>gods = **1 mark** | 2g | 2 |

© Copyright HeadStart Primary Ltd.

## Kites

| No. | Answers and Mark Scheme | Domain | Marks |
|---|---|---|---|
| 1 | perfect | 2a | 1 |
| 2 | silk / paper / (lightweight) bamboo<br>**[Award 1 mark for each correct answer up to a total of 3 marks.]** | 2b | 3 |
| 3 | (flat and) rectangular | 2b | 1 |
| 4 | They might hear the whistles (attached to the kite). | 2d | 1 |
| 5 | The Invention of Kites / Kites in China / Chinese Kites. | 2c | 1 |
| 6 | to carry messages / measure distances / test the strength of the wind / help the Chinese army / send signals during battle<br>**[Award 1 mark for each correct answer up to a total of 3 marks.]** | 2b | 3 |
| 7 | showing how well you fly a kite | 2a | 1 |
| 8 | They provide space on the ground (and in the air). | 2d | 1 |
| 9 | Kites were invented in China. ---------------------- **fact**<br>Kites are flown in the park. ------------------------ **fact**<br>Firehawk is quite hypnotic. ----------------------- **opinion**<br>**[Award 2 marks for three correct answers; 1 mark for two correct answers.]** | 2b | 2 |
| 10 | It suggests the height the kite can reach. | 2g | 1 |
| 11 | better / amazing / superhero / crazy / crafted / dominate / cloud-hugging / hypnotic / dream / jaw-dropping beauty<br>**[Award 1 mark for each correct answer up to a total of 3 marks.]** | 2g | 3 |

| TOTAL | 50 |
|---|---|

© Copyright HeadStart Primary Ltd.

## Street Party

| No. | Answers and Mark Scheme | Domain | Marks |
|---|---|---|---|
| 1 | It is intended to be eye-catching / so that people notice it. | 2g | 1 |
| 2 | all ages / from small children to grandparents / the whole family | 2d | 1 |
| 3 | free / you can give £2 if you wish | 2b | 1 |
| 4 | to celebrate the street being free of cars / traffic / pedestrianised | 2b | 1 |
| 5 | free raffle ticket and a programme | 2b | 1 |
| 6 | They are donating a raffle prize. | 2b | 1 |
| 7 | given | 2a | 1 |
| 8 | 5:30pm | 2b | 1 |
| 9 | Mayor's wife | 2b | 1 |
| 10 | It rhymes. | 2g | 1 |
| 11 | It will be held in the school hall. | 2b | 1 |

**9**

© Copyright HeadStart Primary Ltd.

## Flags and Everything

| No. | Answers and Mark Scheme | Domain | Marks |
|---|---|---|---|
| 1 | Gran | 2d | 1 |
| 2 | school fête / summer fair | 2c | 1 |
| 3 | a (proper) funfair | 2b | 1 |
| 4 | Gran | 2d | 1 |
| 5 | our teacher | 2b | 1 |
| 6 | She is explaining Splat the Rat to someone who might not know how it is played. / It's a joke. | 2d | 1 |
| 7 | She says it was fun. | 2d | 1 |
| 8 | chocolates | 2b | 1 |
| 9 | They are ill. / She says, 'Hope you feel better soon.' | 2d | 1 |
| 10 | Lots of love, Rita x / P.S. at the end / conversational style, i.e. questions, referring to recipient as 'you'. **[Award 2 marks for any two correct answers; 1 mark for one correct answer.]** | 2f | 2 |

© Copyright HeadStart Primary Ltd.

## The Dark Horse

| No. | Answers and Mark Scheme | Domain | Marks |
|---|---|---|---|
| 1 | Jacob | 2f | 1 |
| 2 | He refers to his sister and his sister calls him by name. | 2f | 1 |
| 3 | Thirteen years old | 2b | 1 |
| 4 | stomped | 2g | 1 |
| 5 | candy floss stall | 2b | 1 |
| 6 | homesick | 2b | 1 |
| 7 | sparkling | 2a | 1 |
| 8 | Moonrider | 2b | 1 |
| 9 | It was 'as black as night' [= 1mark] 'with rainbow decorations'. [=1 mark] | 2g | 2 |
| 10 | fly | 2a | 1 |

## The Dark Horse (part 2)

| No. | Answers and Mark Scheme | Domain | Marks |
|---|---|---|---|
| 11 | You don't want that one, lad. = 1 mark<br>Nobody goes on that one. = 1 mark | 2c | 2 |
| 12 | It doesn't earn him any money. | 2d | 1 |
| 13 | fox | 2g | 1 |
| 14 | whirling | 2g | 1 |
| 15 | galloper = 1 mark<br>(wooden) steed = 1 mark | 2a | 2 |
| 16 | people / sideshows / fields<br>**[Award 2 marks for three correct answers; 1 mark for two correct answers.]** | 2b | 2 |
| 17 | carousel / fairground / this new country<br>**[Award 2 marks for three correct answers; 1 mark for two correct answers.]** | 2b | 2 |

© Copyright HeadStart Primary Ltd.

| 18 | hills I used to climb / river I used to swim in / distant snow-capped mountains beyond / our old farm / all the familiar places **[Award 1 mark for each correct answer up to a total of 3 marks.]** | 2c | 3 |
|----|---|---|---|
| 19 | stopped | 2a | 1 |
| 20 | He leaves smiling. | 2d | 1 |
| 21 | Ask for one last ride / ask where the Moonrider came from / ask if he can have it when it is dismantled / try to persuade the owner to keep it. | 2e | 1 |

| | TOTAL | 50 |
|---|---|---|

© Copyright HeadStart Primary Ltd.

**PLEASE NOTE:**

The CD-ROM/digital version also contains the book and tests filed separately for printing.  A full answer version and colour digital versions of the book and tests are also included.

The raw score/scaled score conversion charts are also supplied.